Right to Education through the Lens of Public Administration

Right to Education through the Lens of Public Administration

Dr. Ritesh Kumar Agarwal

GYAN

Published by

Gyan Publishing House
5, Ansari Road
Daryaganj, New Delhi-110002
Phone: 011-47034999, 9811692060
E-mail: books@gyanbooks.com

Distribution Network
gyanbooks.com
India, USA, Canada, UK, Australia, France

ISBN: 978-93-6280-216-3 (HB)

First Published, 2024

Printed at: Gyan Press, Delhi.

Right to Education through the Lens of Public Administration
Author: Dr. Ritesh Kumar Agarwal

Dedicated To My
Revered Parents

Contents

List of Tables

List of Figures

Foreword

Education is a fundamental right vital for the development of individuals and society. While India has made strides in ensuring access to education for all, significant challenges remain. Public administration plays a crucial role in shaping policies and programmes to promote education and ensure it reaches every corner of the nation. Through the public administration lens, we can study the education landscape in India to identify areas for improvement and develop practical solutions to existing challenges. Public administrators can evaluate the role of various stakeholders, including the government, NGOs, and private institutions, in promoting education and provide a roadmap to streamline their efforts for maximum impact. It is crucial to prioritise education in India and ensure that every individual, regardless of background, has access to quality education. The right to education is a cornerstone of a just and equitable society, and public administration can help ensure this right is upheld. A well-planned and executed approach to education can lead to a more educated and skilled workforce, ultimately contributing to the growth and development of the country. In conclusion, public administration is indispensable in promoting education in India. By leveraging its expertise and resources, public administration can help create a comprehensive and effective system that ensures the right to education for all without discrimination

Prof. Abhinav Sharma
Department of Political Science,
Faculty of Social Sciences,
Banaras Hindu University,
Varanasi – 221 005 (U.P.). India.

Preface

Those countries' governments are responsible for fulfilling the needs of the people of any country. The government can be of any kind, such as a parliamentary or presidential system of government. However, one thing that is common in all of these is administration. There is hardly any aspect of life that is not provided by one or more government agencies, i.e., public administration plays the most important role in implementing it.

Public Administration has emerged as an interdisciplinary subject due to the adoption of the Public Policy Approach. Various branches of public administration provide services to society, and educational administration is one of them. Public Administration is concerned with the process and the essential matters of public policy, such as education, health, law and order, agriculture, social security, justice, welfare, etc. Therefore, the strong demand for time makes education the most critical development weapon. Here, we will study the role of administration in primary education, which is one of society's most important tasks.

Developing countries are making concerted efforts to enhance the quality and accessibility of education. Education has gained global recognition as a fundamental human right, empowering individuals with skills, abilities, and confidence to secure other rights. As a key driver of a nation's development, education produces individuals capable of fulfilling diverse societal roles. To ensure the best education, it is imperative to have the most efficient and effective educational administration.

The 86th Constitutional Amendment Act of 2002 marked a significant milestone in public education. This act, which declared free and compulsory primary education for children aged 6 to 14 as a fundamental right under Article 21A, was a game-changer. It was further reinforced by the approval of the 'Right to Free and Compulsory Education Act' by the President of India on 26 August 2009. With the act coming into force on 1 April 2010, India joined the league of 135 countries where education is a fundamental right for its citizens.

For the last few decades, India has emphasised the enrolment rate and school education in primary education. Still, a low learning and dropout rate remains challenging for the central and state governments. The right-to-education approach assumes that the fulfilment of the objective of elementary education includes freedom, rights, and responsibilities, not just a policy goal. Instead of viewing separately, the Right-To-Education approach considered these four dimensions, i.e. availability, affordability, acceptability, and adaptability (4 A's), which influence education. However, the problem is that the context in which all these A's are seen does not include accountability.

The increase in enrollment of children in private schools after implementing the Right to Education Act in 2010 indicates a decrease in the quality of government schools. The need for quality education is in the highest demand for the present situation in the context of an India-like country. Indian government tries to provide all the infrastructural needs for quality and quantitative education, but the dilemma arises when a lacuna is found in the implementation part. Implementation and proper regulation of primary education have become a great challenge for different state governments in India, especially after the Right to Education Act has been passed in Parliament.

The key focus of this book is the role of administration in providing the right to education (RTE) in India. The urban, semi-urban, and remote area, especially with rural backgrounds that lacks basic civic amenities like proper roads, electricity, and water, has a great challenge of fulfilling the population's need for primary education. This book will prove to be helpful for the accessibility of primary education with quality improvements. The present book will focus on four determinants of proper accessibility. In short, it is also known as the 4A criteria (availability, affordability, acceptability, and adaptability) with accountability.

This book attempts to conceptualise access by examining the main constituents of access to primary education. It also attempts to understand the reasons behind low access to elementary education and identify appropriate indicators of the '4A' concept to achieve qualitative educational administration in India.

In the second chapter, an attempt has been made to explain the concept of 4A in elementary education and accountability for qualitative elementary education. In the third chapter, various aspects related to research methodology have been discussed, which mainly includes research methodology in social sciences and public administration as well as qualitative and critical approaches. In the fourth chapter, we will get to know the global perspective of the right to education, which mainly includes Dakar World Education Conference: Education for All, Education for Sustainable Development (ESD), United Nations Millennium Declaration, 2000, Decentralization of Educational Administration in the World, No Child Left Behind (NCLB) Act of America, 2000. The administration of elementary education in India before independence has been explained, under which elementary education in the ancient, Buddhist, Mughal, and British periods has been included. Along with elementary education in India before independence, this chapter includes efforts made by the government for elementary education in India after independence, such as the Kothari Commission (1964-66), National Education Policy (1968, 1986/1992), District Primary Education Programme, Mid-day Meal, Sarva Shiksha Abhiyan (2001), and Early Childhood Care and Education. In the fifth chapter, the Right to Education Act of 2009 and the quality of primary education in India are discussed in detail. In the sixth chapter, based on the information obtained from primary sources, a detailed discussion has been done on the status of the Right to Education in Varanasi. In the seventh chapter, some important recommendations have been made for qualitative improvement in administering the right to education.

The book is the result of my research for PhD in Public Administration. I completed my PhD under the supervision of Prof. Abhinav Sharma from the Department of Political Science at Banaras Hindu University. The present book will serve as a source of information for those researching this area, and graduate and postgraduate students will also benefit from it. Thus, the book presented is important for both researchers and students.

Dr. Ritesh Kumar Agarwal
Postdoctoral Fellow, ICSSR,
Department of Political Science,
Faculty of Social Sciences,
Banaras Hindu University,
Varanasi- 221005 (U.P.). India.

Acknowledgement

I would like to express my deepest gratitude to those who supported me throughout the process of writing this book. Without their guidance, encouragement, and unwavering belief in me, this project would not have been possible.

First and foremost, I am profoundly thankful to my supervisor Prof. Abhinav Sharma, for his invaluable guidance, constructive criticism, and constant support. His insights and expertise have greatly enriched this work, and I am fortunate to have had the opportunity to learn under his mentorship.

I am also deeply appreciative of all the faculty members at the Department of Political Science, Banaras Hindu University, whose knowledge and wisdom have shaped my understanding and approach to this subject. Their dedication to teaching and research has been a source of inspiration.

To my dear friends and colleagues, Dr. Sundhar Vadivu, Dr. Rajesh Kumar, Mr. Brajesh Kumar, Mr. Ashutosh Singh, Dr. Sandeep Singh, Mr. Rohit Balani, Mr. Vishnu Shankar Tiwari, Mr. Rahul Singh, Dr. Vibhooti Narayan, Dr. Amit Kumar Vishwakarma, Dr. Nitesh Thakur, your encouragement and camaraderie have been a source of strength throughout this journey. The late-night discussions, moral support, and shared laughs have been invaluable.

I owe a special debt of gratitude to my parents Mr. Vijay Agarwal and Mrs. Shakuntala Agarwal, whose love, sacrifices, and unwavering belief in me have been my greatest motivation. Your support has been the foundation upon which I have built all my achievements. To my siblings, Mrs. Seema Agarwal, Mrs. Sweta Saraf and Mr. Mukesh Agarwal thank you for being my constant companions and my biggest cheerleaders. Your encouragement and understanding have meant the world to me.

Lastly, I would like to thank everyone else who, in one way or another, contributed to the completion of this book. Your support and belief in my work have been instrumental in making this endeavour a reality.

Dr. Ritesh Kumar Agarwal

Abbreviations

4A	Availability, Affordability, Acceptability, Adaptability
4P	People, Purpose, Performance, Progression
AD	Anno Domini
ASER	Annual Status of Education Report
BC	Before Christ
BPL	Below Poverty Line
DISE	District Information of School Education
DPEP	District Primary Education Programme
ECCE	Early Childhood Care and Education
EFA	Education for All
ESD	Education for Sustainable Development
ICCPR	International Covenant on Civil and Political Rights
ICESCR	International Covenant on Economic, Social and Cultural Rights
MDM	Mid-Day Meal
MHRD	Ministry of Human Resource Development
NCLB	No Child Left Behind
NEP	National Education Policy
NGO	Non-Governmental Organisation
NIEPA	National Institute of Educational Planning and Development
NITI	National Institution for Transforming India
NPEGEL	National Programme for Education of Girls at Elementary Education
NUEPA	National University of Educational Planning and Administration
OECD	Organisation of Economic Cooperation and Development
PISA	Programme for International Student Assessment
PTA	Parent-Teacher Association
RTE	Right to Education
SBI	State Bank of India
SEC	Secondary Education Commission

SEQI	School Education Quality Index
SMC	School Management Committee
SSA	Sarva Shiksha Abhiyan
TLM	Teaching-Learning Material
UDHR	Universal Declaration of Human Rights
UN	United Nations
UNESCO	United Nations Educational, Scientific and Cultural Organisation
UNGA	United Nations General Assembly
UNICEF	United Nations Children's Fund
UP	Uttar Pradesh
US	United States
VMC	Varanasi Municipal Corporation

Introduction

Chapter - I

Introduction

This book unequivocally asserts the pivotal role of administration in establishing and upholding the right to education (RTE). This chapter offers the context of primary education and its significance, which the book discusses and presents. Its purpose is to introduce the background of topics like what administration is and what right to education is and its implication on primary education, followed by a statement of the problem on which its aims and objectives have been charted out. The chapter concludes by providing justifications for undertaking the entire topic and organisation of the book.

1.1. Theoretical Background

1.1.1. Administration

To fulfil the needs of the people of any country, the government of those countries is responsible for it. The government can be of any kind like a Parliamentary system of government, the Presidential system of government, etc. But one thing that is common in all of these is the administration. There is hardly any aspect of life, which one or more governmental agencies are not providing. It is the responsibility of the administration to take care of the people from birth till death.

The word 'administer' is derived from the Latin words 'ad' and 'ministrare', which means 'to serve' or 'to manage'. So, we can use the term 'administration' for 'management of works or affairs', which may be public or private.[1] The administration is responsible for implementing the system more and more efficiently to get maximum output from it. Gladden considers the administration, 'to care for or look after people, to manage

1. Hughes, O. E. (2012). *Public management and administration: An introduction.* Macmillan International Higher Education.

affairs.[1] Nigro considers administration as the utilisation of people and resources,[2] whereas Simon views it as the activities of groups.[3]

1.1.2. Public Administration

The term 'Public' has been incorporated into the administration, depicting the governmental activities of a country, reflecting the broad spectrum of administration. It is present in the context of the distribution of services that separates public administration from private administration. Regarding the distribution of services, we find the public administration very different from the private administration. Public Administration as an academic subject is quite new in the social sciences but as an activity, it is as old as human civilisation is. It is mainly related to compliance with the activities of the government. Along with the rise of the modern welfare state, the work of the state has also increased. Therefore, the state has become an important part of the survival of life because it helps society unite for the common interest and makes its achievement easier.

We can understand the term public administration in two senses, i.e. wider or broader sense and narrower sense. In a wider sense, public administration deals with all three branches of government, i.e. legislative, executive, and judiciary supported by Woodrow Wilson, Pfiffner, Marshall Dimock, L.D. White, and F.A. Nigro. In a narrower sense, public administration deals only with the government's executive branch, supported by Fayol, Ordway Tead, Gullick, Simon, and Willoughby.[4]

Woodrow Wilson considers public administration to be the detailed and systematic execution of the law.[5] At the same time, L. D. White believes that the objective of public administration is the fulfilment or enforcement of the public policy,[6] whereas Dwight Waldo sees public administration as the art and science of management that aims to implement the affairs of the state.[7]

---

1. Gladden, E. N. (2019). *A History of Public Administration: Volume I: From the Earliest Times to the Eleventh Century*. Routledge.
2. Nigro, L. G., Nigro, F. A., & Kellough, J. E. (2012). *The new public personnel administration*. Cengage Learning.
3. Simon, H. A. (2013). *Administrative behavior*. Simon and Schuster.
4. Sapru, R. K. (2008). *Administrative theories and management thought*. PHI Learning Pvt. Ltd.
5. Wilson, W. (1955). *The study of public administration* (Vol. 744, No. 24). Public Affairs Press.
6. Basu, R. (1994). *Public administration: Concepts and theories*. Sterling Publishers Pvt. Ltd.
7. Waldo, D. (2006). *The administrative state: A study of the political theory of American public administration*. Transaction Publishers.

It is necessary to note here that Willoughby has differentiated between executive power and administrative power and added the term 'administration' to the administrative branch only, i.e. the fourth branch of government. The importance of public administration can be understood through the points given below:

1. Scientific and technological development has significantly increased the work of government, through which the continuous increase in the role of administration can be seen.
2. Due to the increasing socio-economic problems through the industrial revolution, the responsibilities of the government have greatly increased.
3. With the fulfilment of basic needs, the role of the government has also increased due to the establishment of a Welfare State.
4. Due to the adoption of economic planning by modern governments for the welfare state's objectives, the role of public administration is also increasing.
5. Due to population explosion, slum growth, lack of grains, the problem of transportation, etc. can be seen, which can be redressed mainly by the public administration.
6. Due to modern warfare, the importance of public administration can also be seen in the mobilisation of human and material resources.
7. Increasing the functions of public administration are also seen as also for rescue operations during various calamities such as floods, drought, earthquakes, etc.
8. When there is a decline in social harmony and an increase in violence, public administration is still needed for crisis management.
9. Meeting the needs of the present without compromising on future capabilities is a sign of sustainable development.

Public Administration deals with every aspect of human life. Public Administration is not only related to process but also related to the important matters of administration, such as education, health, law and order, agriculture, social security, justice, welfare, etc. Here, we will explore the role of administration in primary education, which is one of society's most critical responsibilities.

1.1.3. Public Policy Approach

Public Administration has emerged as an interdisciplinary subject due to the adoption of the Public Policy Approach. Various branches of public administration are involved in providing services to the society and educational administration is one of them.

As it is claimed, for the implementation of rules and laws adopted by the legislature, executive, and judiciary, public administration involves all individuals, processes, and organisations together and public administration is everywhere. Yet it can be said that public administration has ignored public education.[1] While it is believed that public administration is concerned with the management of public programmes.[2]

1.1.4. Education

Education is the basic means of human development. By this, society and nation all develop. Ideas such as justice, freedom, and peace can be developed in society only through the spread of education. Therefore, education is the most important resource in the modern life system, through which the person obtains knowledge. In its absence the person is incomplete. Therefore, making education the most important tool for development is a strong demand of our time. New ideas are born through education. Thus, society is created by education itself. According to Locke, "The development of plants is achieved through agriculture, and human development is accomplished through education."[3] The importance of literacy cannot be denied by the economy either. It has been seen that the state of high literacy states is very good in the economy compared to low literacy states.

Education as a key parameter in a Nation's development is responsible for providing the requisite number and quality of persons required to perform varied roles in society. The degree of development of any society is judged by its literacy rate and more prominently any democratic society needs more of its people educated. To achieve this objective, it is pertinent that education should be at its best to reach out to society and simultaneously society should make most from the education be it at any level. To have the best education, there is a dire need to have the most efficient and effective educational administration. It has been appropriately

1. Raffel, J. A. (2007). *Why has public administration ignored public education, and does it matter?* Public Administration Review, 67(1), 135-151.
2. Denhardt, R. B., & Grubbs, J. W. (2003). *Public administration: An action orientation* (p. 36). United States: Thomson and Wadsworth.
3. Pierce, C. (2012). *Education in the age of bio capitalism: Optimizing educational life for a flat world.* Springer.

pointed out that "structurally administration is seen as the hierarchy of superior-subordinate relationship within the social system".

1.1.5. Educational Administration

Various branches of public administration offer a wide range of services to society, and 'educational administration' is one of them. Educational administration helps to spread education that in turn develops the overall personality of an individual and makes him productive for society. Therefore, studying the role of education and education administration is significant for assessing national development.

Educational administration can be understood in the sense that the goal of education is achieved through effective and efficient processes of inputs available to it. In the context of education, this concept is directly linked to the effective utilisation of the various accessible resources within the environment. This utilisation is pivotal in attaining the objectives of both teaching and learning. It is based on the basic principles of human relations and is concerned with the management of things as well as the purpose of educating children and youth. Thus, the optimal functioning of the institution as well as educational administration works to develop the human personality in a balanced way.

1.1.6. About Primary Education

The first level of a formal education system is called primary education. Primary education is the initial stage and the foundation of formal education, playing a crucial role in the socialisation process of the child. Due to being the basic pillar of formal education, it seems more appropriate to give the name of primary education. The education given to children from 6 years to 14 years is covered under primary education which runs from class 1 to class 8. In the progress of any country, the education system holds an important place. This is the first staircase that successfully crosses the goal of a person, society, or nation by progressively reaching its desired goal.

In India, the first level of a formal education system is called primary education which is given after preschool and before secondary education. Primary education, also known as elementary education in India, begins at the age of six.

1.1.7. 86th Constitutional Amendment Act, 2002

Education was included in the state list at the time of implementation of the constitution in India, but since 1977 it has been included in the concurrent list and now it is a joint responsibility of the central and state governments, they try their level of development for education. A variety of efforts are underway by the Central and State Governments to provide free and compulsory education to all children aged 6 to 14, such as the 86th Constitutional Amendment Act of 2002. In the direction of public education, the 86th Constitutional Amendment Act, of 2002 proved to be the milestone, according to which free and compulsory primary education for children between the ages of 6 and 14 years has been made the fundamental right under Article 21A so that they cannot be denied.[1] For the substitution of the new article of article 45, the state shall endeavour to provide childhood care and education to the children until they reach the age of six. In article 51A of the Constitution, the clause "k" shall be added, namely, providing opportunities for education of children by parents or wards, as the case may be, of 6 to 14-year-old children.[2]

1.1.8. Right to Education (RTE) Act, 2009

The "Right to Free and Compulsory Education Act" was approved by the President of India on 26 August 2009. When the Act came into force on 1 April 2010, India became one of the 135 countries where education was accepted as a fundamental right for its citizens.[3]

The implementation of the Right to Education Act can be seen in different parts of the country with some differences. In several states, the implementation of this legislation has been successful in ensuring the right to education. However, in some states, it has not been effectively carried out, thereby failing to fulfil its intended purpose. It is broadly believed that the main reason behind these differences is that in villages, cities, and districts where economic, political, social, etc., backwardness is present, it is proving difficult to implement this law. When examining the underdevelopment of these areas in terms of resource availability, we find that the lack of access to primary education and essentials such as food, housing, and healthcare are significant factors. The absence of these resources also discourages qualified teachers and administrators from performing their roles effectively in these areas.

1.2. Research Problem

For the last few decades, India has emphasised the enrolment rate and school education in primary education, but a low level of learning and

1. The Constitution (Eighty-Sixth Amendment) Act, (2002). National Portal of India, 2012. Retrieved from https://www.india.gov.in/my-government/constitution-india/amendments/constitution-india-eighty-sixth-amendment-act-2002
2. Jain, S. C. (2002). *The Constitution (Eighty-Sixth Amendment) Act.* New Delhi: Government of India.
3. Puar, S. S. (2012). *Right to Education Act: A critical analysis.* International Journal of Educational and Psychological Research (IJEPR), 1(2), 27-30.

dropout rate remains a challenge for the central and state governments.[1] Currently, there are about 94 lakh children who have either dropped out of school or never attended school.[2]

Problems arising out of the absence of elementary education do not end here. According to UNICEF, in 2011, about 10.1 million children of 5 to 14 years in India are working.[3] According to various institutions, any child who does not attend school is child labour.

The concept of access is rather abstract and the available literature has so far failed to devise a means to identify suitable indicators. There are two points of confusion for access, conceptualising access i.e., deciding what constitutes access, and second, after identifying the indicators, can accountability be included.

The right-to-education approach assumes that the fulfilment of the objective of elementary education includes freedom, rights, and responsibilities, not just a policy goal. According to former UN special rapporteur Katarina Tomasevski on the Right to Education Act, the right to education can be seen as the 4A scheme, that is, availability, accessibility, acceptability, and adaptability should be structured as indicators of education.[4] Accessibility can also be seen as affordability.

If we look at the first problem, i.e. conceptualising access then, officially, access is seen from the perspective of availability and affordability. Under the right to education, it is the effort of the government that in the process of access, the first resource should be available, and then it should be made free. This makes it easier for disadvantaged groups as well as all people to access primary education by building new schools and meeting the direct economic costs of education. But in addition to availability and affordability, it encourages researchers to look for other indicators for access.

The *availability* of resources is the first determinant of achieving the right to education. Thinkers have also tried to explain through their articles that the availability of various resources is the main determinant of

1. Sahni, U. (2015). *Primary education in India: Progress and challenges*. The second Modi-Obama summit: Building the India-US partnership, 35-38.
2. Singh, J. (2014). *Article 21A (Right to education): Critical analysis*. Asian Journal of Multidimensional Research (AJMR), 3(3), 45-50.
3. Child labour and exploitation. (2011). Unicef India. Retrieved from https://www.unicef.org/india/what-we-do/child-labour-exploitation
4. Tomasevski, K. (2001). *Human rights obligations: making education available, accessible, acceptable and adaptable*. Raoul Wallenberg Institute of Human Rights and Humanitarian Law.

attainment. (Tilak, 1996)[1] (Dreze & Kingdon, 1999), etc. has identified a positive relationship between the availability of basic facilities in schools and enrolment of children.[2]

Along with the availability of resources, its *affordability* is also seen as a major indicator of the right to education. At various times, the government has tried to free its resources to increase access to the school, such as free education, textbooks, mid-day meals, etc. According to Buckland (2000)[3] and Mehrotra and Panchmukhi (2006), it was discovered that families with children attending private schools experienced a greater financial strain compared to those with children in government schools.[4] In such a situation, only small children are the source of their parents' financial needs. In such a situation, confusion arises in front of parents because on one hand there is a lack of quality education in government schools, and on the other hand there is a lack of financial resources as well as the financial burden of sending children to private schools.

Sometimes it happens that the person is in a position to get benefits in terms of availability and strength, but due to lack of adaptability of the education provider's attitude and receiver, the person gets denied. Therefore, it can be assumed that not only the affordability of access but also the correct attitude of the provider and the adaptability of the receiver should also be seen as essential indicators for access.

Vasavi (2006) views access from the angle of *acceptability*.[5] To encourage the participation of students from all social inter-classes and to ensure their admission in schools, education providers and administrators must remove prejudice and biased attitudes towards them. If the behaviour of the teacher and the administrator is harmful to the children of the disadvantaged class, then it will keep the students away from getting an education. The time demands that teachers, administrators, and students should not keep negative feelings in their minds toward the children of the disadvantaged class. Due to disparity in distribution and discriminatory attitudes of providers, underprivileged children face a variety of problems.

1. Tilak, J. B. (1996). *How free is 'free' primary education in India?* Economic and Political Weekly, 355-366.
2. Dreze, J., & Kingdon, G. G. (1999). *School Participation in Rural India: The Development Economics Discussion Paper Series, No. 18.* London: London School of Economics.
3. Buckland, P. (2000). *Making quality basic education affordable: what have we learned?* New York: UNICEF Cameron.
4. Mehrotra, S., & Panchamukhi, P. R. (2006). *Private provision of elementary education in India: Findings of a survey in eight states.* Compare, 36(4), 421-442.
5. Vasavi, A. R. (2006). *Caste indignities and subjected personhoods.* Economic and Political Weekly, 3766-3771.

Sometimes a common mainstream language is used by teachers for all children and poor children are given less attention, i.e., due to the negative attitude of the teachers, poor or deprived children feel weak in education. To fulfil the objective of the right to education, it is seen as a challenge to overcome problems like social hierarchy, etc. In such a situation, improvement in the attitude and behaviour of teachers and administrators becomes very necessary for qualitative primary education.

Govinda (2008) and others found that *adaptability* is also an important determinant of children's access to primary education.[1] The desire, attitude, and motivation of the recipients of education have also been considered to be very important for elementary education. According to Dreze & Sen (1995) and other researchers, parents are discouraged from supporting their children's education due to factors beyond financial costs. These factors include preparing children for school, providing encouragement, assisting with homework, and fostering positive relationships with teachers.[2] Adaptability to education also depends on the fact that parents do not make any distinction between sons and daughters, should not think of boys as breadwinners and girls as housekeepers only, but rather encourage both boys and girls to go to school with the same vision. And it is also necessary for parents to remove their hesitation for the education of daughters in co-educational schools. Unless parents send children to school, it will be difficult to universalise education, no matter what facilities and resources are available related to the school. For this, the education provider must repeatedly prove the productivity of education to parents. Keeping these indicators in mind, we need to identify other indicators and develop them as concepts of accessibility.

The second problem relates to administrative accountability, i.e. accountability should be seen as the key to a successful school system and it should be fair and transparent.[3] Public Accountability is the pivot of public administration in democracy. Public Administration is indirectly responsible to the public through the political executive, legislative judiciary, etc. Supervisory personnel are confined primarily to administrative inspections and data gathering. In small cities, semi-urban, and remote areas in India, local communities lack the expertise to evaluate teachers and administrators professionally.

---

1. Govinda, R. & Bandyopadhyay, M. *Achieving Universal Elementary Education in India: Expanding Access with Equity.* NUEPA, New Delhi, 1-37.
2. Dreze, J., & Sen, A. (1999). *India: Economic development and social opportunity.* Oxford University Press Catalogue.
3. Cheminais, R. (2014). *Special educational needs for qualified and trainee teachers: A practical guide to the new changes.* Routledge.

The comprehensive right-to-education approach considers four significant dimensions (which are referred to as the 4 A's) that profoundly impact education, rather than treating them as separate entities. But the problem is that the context in which all these A's are seen is not in terms of accountability.

1.2.1. About Varanasi

In the context of this study, the empirical research aims at enhancing the understanding of the shortcomings of the provision of the right to education in the area under the study. The study would propose suggestions on how accountability can be utilised to improve the state of accountable educational administration in the city of Varanasi.

The City of Varanasi (also known as Banaras or Kashi) is one of the oldest living cities in the world.[1] It is worshipped as one of the most ancient cultural and sacred cities of India. According to the 2011 census, the population of Varanasi stands at 36,76,841.[2] There are a total of 90 wards under the Varanasi Municipal Corporation spread over an area of 79.79 sq. / km. Rapid unplanned urbanisation, and economic growth combined with huge tourist flows and floating populations have also put enormous pressure on the city's education system.

The most important reason for choosing Varanasi City is the falling quality of elementary education here. According to the survey conducted by the Annual Status of Education Report (ASER) 2014, important points of elementary education of the Varanasi division have been shown. The increase in enrollment of children in private schools after the implementation of the Right to Education Act in the year 2010 indicates a decrease in the quality of government schools. During the year 2010-14, the increase in enrollment of children in private schools increased from 42.21% to about 57.54%. The number of children of classes 1-2 who can read the letter has decreased from 82.9% in the year 2010 to 70.23% in the year 2014. The number of children of class 1-2 who can recognize the number of 1-9 has come down from 78.73% in the year 2010 to 73.58% in the year 2014. The number of children of class 3-5 who can read the books of class 1 has come down from 68.4% in the year 2010 to just 55.52% in the year 2014.[3] The

1. Jha, D., & Tripathi, V. (2014). *Quality of life in slums of Varanasi city: a comparative study*. Transactions, 36(2).
2. Varanasi District Population Census, (2011-2020). Uttar Pradesh literacy, sex ratio and density, 2011. Retrieved from https://www.census2011.co.in/census/district/568-varanasi.html
3. ASER (Annual Status of Education Report), 2014.

number of children of class 3-5 who can do subtraction has come down from 51.06% in the year 2010 to just 42.9% in the year 2014.[1]

According to ASER 2018, at Varanasi, the percentage of children in classes 3 to 5 who can read class 2 level texts in the year 2018 is only 50.8%. The percentage of children in classes 6 to 8 who can divide in the year 2018 is only 41.8%.

1.3. Objectives

The present book focuses on the following objectives:

1. To conceptualize access i.e., examine the main constituents of access to primary education.
2. To develop suitable indicators of availability, affordability, acceptability, and adaptability.
3. To identify the indicators (among 4 A's) that are responsible for low access in the Varanasi of Uttar Pradesh.
4. To identify the possibilities of an accountable educational administration.

It is; therefore, the present analysis seeks to examine:

1. How access could be conceptualised in terms of four indicators availability, affordability, acceptability, and adaptability?
2. How to develop different indicators of these 4 A's?
3. Whether there is accountability in educational administration?
4. We can measure accountability at the Uttar Pradesh level with the help of secondary data, and if yes, can we compare it with the Varanasi level?

1.4. Hypothesis/Hypotheses

A hypothesis is a complete, efficient, proposed, and testable statement based on the assumption of two or more variables that tell us what we want to see. The following hypotheses are given by the author for the present study.

1. Access to primary education can be seen in terms of the four A's namely- availability, affordability, acceptability, and adaptability.
2. The 4A's mentioned above can be improved with some indicators.
3. The 4A's mentioned above can be conceptualised with accountability.

1. ASER (Annual Status of Education Report), 2015.

4. Low achievement on accountability is responsible for low access to primary education in Varanasi.

1.5. Justification for Study

The need for quality education is in the highest demand for the present situation in the context of an India-like country. Indian government tries to provide all the infrastructural needs for quality and quantitative education but the dilemma arises when it is found lacuna in the implementation part. Implementing and properly regulating primary education has become a great challenge for different state governments in India, especially after the Right to Education Act was passed in Parliament. The urban, semi-urban, and remote area, especially with rural backgrounds that lacks basic civic amenities like proper roads, electricity, and water, has a great challenge of fulfilling the needs of the population for primary education. This book will prove to be helpful for the accessibility of primary education with quality improvements. This book will focus on the determinants of proper accessibility which are four in number in short it is also known as the 4A criteria (availability, affordability, acceptability, and adaptability) with accountability.

1.6. Organisation of the Book

This book is comprised of seven chapters, details of which are outlined as follows:

Chapter 1: Introduction

This chapter first provides the context of the study and problem of primary education on which the whole book is discussed and presented. This chapter intends to introduce the background of the study, what public administration is, why public administration, what right to education (RTE) is and its implication on a child's future and public life, and the rationale for administration in the provision of the right to education, etc. which is followed by the statement of the problem on which aims and objectives of the book have been charted out. This chapter has been concluded by providing justifications for undertaking this study and the organisation of the book.

Chapter 2: Enhancing Educational Administration: The 4A Concept and Accountability

In this chapter, the theoretical underpinnings of this research work have been dealt which throws light on the concept of 4A and accountability, the role of educational administration, issues and challenges, and the way it is being managed. The relationship between accountability and educational administration is discussed. Various measures of accountability have also been dealt with along with their respective strengths and weaknesses. The rationale for using accountability has been elucidated in detail followed by its limitations highlighted by academicians and researchers across the world. In this chapter, an endeavour has been made to examine the literature available in the form of books, articles, and reports on the study area.

Chapter 3: Research Methodology in Public Administration

This chapter aims to present a conceptual framework of public administration in the delivery of public infrastructure and service. This chapter focuses on the concepts and methods relevant to an empirical study on the 'Right to Education through the Lens of Public Administration'. The aim is to conduct an empirical study to collect and analyse data on the state of the right to education, satisfaction, the attitude of teachers and parents of children towards RTE, suitable indicators of primary education, and possibilities of an accountable educational administration. For this, various research methodological concerns have been dealt with in this chapter to identify a research method that is most appropriate for the study.

Chapter 4: Right to Education: A Global Perspective

This chapter shows the role of administration in the right to education at the global level. It also discusses the various measures taken to promote education at different stages in India's history. Through this chapter, we can gain insight into the criteria that can be utilised to enhance the right to education in India.

Chapter 5: Right to Education and Quality of Primary Education in India

In this chapter, details of the Right to Education Act of 2009 have been discussed. The plight of the Right to Education across India has also been presented. Different flaws and deficiencies of administrative practices have also been highlighted coupled with the status of the Right to Education in India.

Chapter 6: Status of Right to Education in Varanasi

The previous chapter presented a conceptual framework and a basis for undertaking empirical research on the theme of this book. Consequently, the purpose of this chapter is to systematically present and analyse data collected to the extent to determine the attitude and perspective of parents of the children and teachers and administrators of the school on the Right to Education. It also aimed at finding problems with RTE along with respondents' suggestions on how to improve primary education in the city under study. This empirical study is based on data collected from 351 respondents from the city of Varanasi through the interview schedule.

Chapter 7: Summary of Findings and Recommendations

This chapter aims to examine the objectives of the book like: (a) to conceptualise access i.e. examine the main constituents of access to primary education. (b) to develop suitable indicators of availability, affordability, acceptability, and adaptability. (c) to identify the indicators (among 4 A's) that are responsible for low access in the Varanasi district of Uttar Pradesh. (d) to identify the possibilities of an accountable educational administration. The main summary of the findings and recommendations is presented in this chapter.

Enhancing Educational Administration: The 4A Concept and Accountability

Chapter - II

Enhancing Educational Administration: The 4A Concept and Accountability

2.1. About Human Development

Education is the basic means of human development. By this, society and nation all develop. Ideas such as justice, freedom, and peace can be created in society only through the spread of education. Therefore, education is the most important resource in the modern life system, through which the person obtains knowledge. In its absence the person is incomplete. Hence, the strong demand for time makes education the most important development weapon. New ideas are born through education, so a good society is created by education itself. The importance of literacy cannot be denied by the economy either. It has been seen that the state of high literacy states is very good compared to low literacy states.

2.2. About School

The school is a formal organisation and it is also called a social organisation. This is the appropriate place where knowledge of the art of living in life is provided. Accountability also properly guides us to make this work vigorously. The work of the school is involved in accountability. Through this, each employee is dedicated to his organisation. Accountability keeps the worker alert toward his liability. At the same time emphasizes each task in a very conscious and ordered form.

Based on the findings of the Secondary Education Commission (1952-1953), it is undeniable that a school plays a crucial role as an educational institution. The teacher's primary responsibility is to shape students' personalities to ensure their physical health, mental awareness, emotional stability, cultural strength, and social competence. This will only be possible if the manager, principal, teachers, and other staff can fulfil their responsibility for proper accountability. Accountability is the state of being held responsible and legally obligated to fulfil one's duties.[1]

In the new education policy (1986, 1992), teachers are expected to demonstrate high levels of performance, dedication, and commitment to their profession. Many commissions such as the University Commission (1948), Mudaliar Education Commission (1952-53), Kothari Commission (1964-66), and the National Education Policy (1968) have made suggestions on teachers' responsibilities. Much responsibility for the success or failure of the education system depends on the teachers.

Today the field of teacher's role has expanded, whether education is related to any level but elementary education is the stage of life where the journey of child development begins. But today the need to achieve the goal of primary-level public education of elementary education has attracted to the responsibilities of teachers at this level.

After independence, efforts were made to improve elementary education through various policies at different times, including the education policies of 1968, 1986, 1992, etc. In 1976, education was transferred to the concurrent list, after which efforts were made by the state governments as well as the central government to improve education.[2] In this regard, we can see the Sarva Shiksha Abhiyan 2001, 86th Constitutional Amendment (Right to Education) 2002, and the Right to Education Act of 2009 marked the most significant step in the field of elementary education at the beginning of the 21st century.

2.3. Educational Administration

Education is considered one of the most important factors of development. The future of the country significantly depends on the advancement of Indian education. This underscores the immense importance of focusing on the development of the education system.[3]

At present, the term educational administration is used extensively. Educational administration encompasses a wide range of responsibilities such as strategizing, coordinating, overseeing, and regulating educational

---

1. Tilak, J. B. (1988). *Vocational education in South Asia: Problems and prospects.* International Review of Education, 244-257.
2. Bakshi, P. M. (2013). *Concurrent powers of legislation under List III of the Constitution.* Ministry of Law and Justice. Accessed on June, 9, 2014.
3. Naik, J. P. (1965). *Educational planning in India.* Allied Publishers.

activities. It requires a combination of innate talent, specialised training, extensive knowledge, and practical experience.[1]

Mathur (1983), described three processes of planning in his book, 'Towards Improved Educational Planning and Administration' and says planning involves three major processes which may, in general terms be referred to as the political process, the technical process, and the administrative process.

(a) In the realm of politics, the process involves the creation of goals, which essentially means outlining the specific directions in which a nation is envisioned to progress.

(b) The technical process involves the detailed analysis and deconstruction of overarching goals into specific operational objectives. This is followed by the formulation of a comprehensive plan of action that outlines the steps to be taken to achieve those objectives.

(c) The administrative process involves overseeing and implementing the designed plan of action. Formulation of rules and regulations to promote those individual and social behaviours that further, and prevent that which hamper, the realisation of the plan goals, is a part of this process. Evaluation of the implementation of various programs could partly be undertaken as an administrative activity, although it is also a part of the technical process.[2]

The planning process, as defined above, may diagrammatically be represented as follows:-

Political Process **Technical Process** **Administrative process**

Goal Setting...............Plan Formulation............. Implementation

↑ ....Evaluation.............................. ↑

According to **(Mathur, 1983),** the administration of today is a challenging task. It not only requires technical know-how but also practical human skills. There are detailed volumes written on the scientific analysis of administration and technical functions of an administrator, but every administrator knows that practical human qualities are also essential for the successful operation of an organisation. Hence, administration is

1. Gaind, D. N., & Sharma, R. P. (1966). *Education and Secondary School Administration.* Ram Prasad.
2. Mathur, M. V. (1983). *Towards Improved Educational Planning and Administration.* Joy Madhathi Kunnel for Dialogue, New Delhi.

an art everyone has to learn on the job. Therefore, beyond managerial qualifications obtained from a school, college, or university, the modern administrator needs specific human qualities and leadership skills to effectively manage human organisations. Educational institutions, truthfully speaking, are more human-centric than many others because they prepare and train individuals for society at large.[1]

Bhagia et al., (1990) in their book, 'Educational Administration in India and Other Developing Countries, pp. 10' say educational administration and elementary education that, the lower level of literacy in most developing countries can be attributed to the high rate of population growth and the correspondingly slow rate of coverage of elementary and education accompanied by a high drop-out rate at the elementary stage of education.

Bhagia et al., (1990) in their book, 'Educational Administration in India and Other Developing Countries, pp. 35-36' Glueck, (1974) stated that training could reduce waste, increase output, reduce equipment maintenance, and improve quality output. While training is not solely responsible for all of those improvements, it could contribute to both the efficiency and the effectiveness of goals. The process of training plays a crucial role in psychology as it facilitates employees in effectively adapting to their work environment.[2]

Bhagia et al., (1990) in their book, 'Educational Administration in India and Other Developing Countries, Pg.30', about educational administration, major weaknesses in educational administration in developing countries are largely related to personnel management. These include unsatisfactory methods of recruitment, inadequate provision of training, lack of specialised staff, poor service conditions of employees, and lack of welfare schemes. One of the conclusions of a recent diagnostic study of educational administration sponsored by the UNESCO Regional Office, Bangkok, was that there was substantial scope for improving some of the practices related to personnel management, such as frequent transfer opportunities for career development, and continuous performance appraisal.[3]

Mishra (2007) says in his book, that in the schools, human relations are more important. Narrow-minded clerks are not required in educational

1. Mathur, M. V. (1983). *Towards Improved Educational Planning and Administration*. Joy Madhathi Kunnel for Dialogue, New Delhi.
2. Glueck, W. F. (1974). *Personnel: A diagnostic approach*. Business Publications.
3. Bhagia, N., Briggs, D., & Bhagia, S. (1990). *Educational administration in India and other developing countries: Challenges, tasks and training*. Commonwealth Publishers. p. 30.

institutions. Self-centred and selfish people will not prove to be good for the school climate. A good person and open-minded person will be better for raising young children like budding flowers. Those who understand the innocence of children and the feelings of people can prove capable of enriching any school or institution with their contribution. R. C. Mishra views educational administration from the angle of human relationships, he says, that educational administration is concerned with the management of things as well as with human relationships i.e. the better working together of people. It is more related to humans and less to inanimate things. It is, therefore, primarily a social enterprise.[1]

According to the author in the Journal **(Kurukshetra, May 2011)**, the government has tried to encourage the development of education from policymaking to law enforcement, but implementing it effectively is still a big challenge.

Malan (1987) in their book about the decentralisation of educational administration says the French Ninth Plan (1984-1988) represents a new step forward in articulation between national and regional planning and which is based on an important phase of the decentralisation process. The key innovation involves the implementation of a system of "planning contracts" between the central government and regional authorities. These contracts allow individual regions to establish agreements with the central government for the development and execution of their plans in collaboration.[2]

Mwinjuma (2015) talks about autonomy for decentralisation and that, many countries of the world have implemented reforms in various ways, in which the concept of autonomy and empowerment can be seen as the main features of decentralised schools[3] and at the same time reflect the high autonomy level achieved by the headmaster.[4]

Jha et al., (2013) in their study talk about decentralised tribunals and say, that most states do not have any system of decentralised tribunals to address various teacher-related issues. Teacher accountability is another side of teacher motivation.[5]

---

1. Mishra, R. C. (2007). *History of education administration*. APH Pub.
2. Malan, T. (1987). *Educational planning as a social process* (No. 33-37). Unipub.
3. Mwinjuma, J. S. (2015). *A Review of Characteristics and Experiences of Decentralisation of Education.* International Journal of Education and Literacy Studies, 3(1), 34-41.
4. Santiago, P., McGregor, I., Nusche, D., Ravela, P., & Toledo, D. (2012). *OECD Reviews of Evaluation and Assessment in Education: Mexico.* OECD Publishing.
5. Jha, J., Ghatak, N., Chandrashekaran, S., Mahendiran, S., Minni, P., Bakshi, S., & Thyagrajan, R. (2013). *Challenges in Implementing the Right to Education: The Karnataka Case.* Centre for Budget and Policy Studies Working Paper.

2.3.1. Objectives of Educational Administration

(a) Administration to provide proper education to students

Proper education should not be construed to mean that it speaks of expensive or high-cost education. Rather it means providing proper education within a reasonable cost i.e. qualitative improvement along with quantitative expansion.

(b) Using resources adequately and appropriately

There is a need to ensure adequate use of human, material, and financial resources for the achievement of educational objectives.

(c) Professionalising the ethics and development of teachers

Since teachers are directly connected to children and parents, their role is very important for access to education. Teachers should be encouraged to participate in service education programmes along with developing new ideas. There is also a need to make teachers aware of hard work, dedication, and commitment to their work to achieve the objectives of educational administration.

(d) Organising programmes to make children democratic citizens

To organise programmes to make children democratic citizens as well as to provide them with the art and training of living.

(e) Developing relationships with the community and uniting them

Educational administration should emphasize that along with quantitative expansion of education; obtain community support for qualitative development and smooth and fair conduct of examination.

(f) Organising co-curricular activities for teachers and students

Organising co-curricular activities to develop the child's talent along with the efficiency of teachers.

(g) To complete the work effectively

The most important objective of educational administration is to implement the tasks effectively and efficiently to benefit the individual and society.

(h) Preparing students for the future

Along with education, students need to be trained in such a way that they can use their talent in various jobs, businesses, and other occasions.

(i) To develop scientific vision in students

A major objective of educational administration is also to develop a scientific attitude towards all aspects of life in the minds of children.

(j) Qualitative improvement in teaching as well as education

To meet the objectives of qualitative education and proper teaching, the educational administration must ensure regular supervision of teaching and guidance of teachers.

2.4. The Concept of 4A

Tomasevski (2006) provided a thematic framework for understanding the rights-based approach to education, which is both useful and informative.[1] The right to education focuses on areas like availability, affordability, acceptability adaptability, etc.

2.4.1. Availability

Availability of basic resources is the main determinant of access to education. For enrolment/retention, it is important to make resources available in schools. Lack of teachers' effort, lack of availability of books, and lack of teaching and learning materials, etc. are the main causes of the obstacles to quality education in India.

According to **Spreen and Valley (2006)**, the right to education, along with being a multiplier, protects all individual rights and freedoms, and where the rights and freedoms of the deprived are violated, the right to education is effectively, guaranteed.[2]

In the Journal **(Kurukshetra, May 2011)** Hazra talks about 'Availability of Resources' for education in a government-aided primary school in India. According to the author, children in rural areas continue to be deprived of quality education owing to factors like a lack of competent and committed teachers, a lack of textbooks or teaching-learning materials, and so on. The much-publicized mid-day meal (MDM) scheme meant to reduce drop-out rates in schools seems to be not yielding the desired results due to the alleged misappropriation of funds.[3]

2.4.2. Affordability

According to **Tomaskveski (2006)**, dealing with exclusion requires

---

1. Klees, S. J., & Thapliyal, N. (2007). *The right to education: The work of Katarina Tomasevski.* Comparative Education Review, 51(4), 497-510.
2. Spreen, C. A., &Vally, S. (2010). *Prospects and pitfalls: A review of post-apartheid education policy research and analysis in South Africa.* Comparative Education, 46(4), 429-448.
3. Hazra, A. (May 2011). *The Challenge of Educating Rural India.* Kurukshetra, 59(7), 3-5.

not only combating its effects but also reversing and stopping exclusionary practices and policies.[1]

An approach based on rights emphasizes the importance of taking into account the specific needs of each child and guaranteeing that education is not just offered, but also within reach for all.[2] The rights-based approach to education is also important from an equity perspective because it assumes that all children with equal access to different abilities and resources are unable to enter schools. To ensure the effective implementation of the right to education, it is essential to have a comprehensive understanding of multiple relevant facts and considerations.

2.4.3. Acceptability

Children should have the right to be treated fairly and equally, without facing any discrimination. Individuals need to have the chance to engage meaningfully in their communities and to receive a high-quality education.[3] "Students should be ready to take on responsibilities as parents and participate in political processes. They should also be equipped to contribute to social unity and to instil in young people the belief that everyone, including themselves, has the right to be treated as a human being."[4]

Mishra (2007) in his book says about acceptability, i.e., relationship in school that, in schools, the relationship of teachers and administrators with children and their parents holds a very important place in the development of education. Some Heads knowingly create groups in the staff and some others try to make the teachers individual-minded. It is often seen that administrators take little interest in keeping all the employees of the organisation united and integrated. In educational institutions like these, the teachers have a strong camaraderie, and they genuinely relish spending time with their students.[5]

Govinda and Bandyopadhyay (2008), in their book, talk about the teachers' attitude toward children and say, that the social distance between

1. Klees, S. J., & Thapliyal, N. (2007). *The right to education: The work of Katarina Tomasevski.* Comparative Education Review, 51(4), 497-510.
2. UNICEF. (2007). *A human rights-based approach to education for all: A framework for the realisation of children's right to education and rights within education.* United Nations Publications.
3. Craissati, D. (2007). *A human rights-based approach to education for all: a framework for the realisation of children's right to education and rights within education.* New York: United Nations Children's Fund.
4. Tomasevski, Katarina. (2003). *Education denied: costs and remedies.* New York: Zed Books.
5. Mishra, R. C. (2007). *History of education administration.* APH Pub. pp. 49-50.

teachers and students is one reason why many teachers have a low interest in the pupils' education and a low understanding of pupils' problems.

2.4.4. Adaptability

Bhagia et al., (1990) in their book, 'Educational Administration in India and Other Developing Countries, p. 172' talk about adaptability and say, that adaptability is the degree to which an innovation can be changed and adapted according to institutional or local needs. An innovation ordinarily must be modified somewhat to meet the requirements of a local institution. This is true almost always when a school or school system adopts any type of change. Such factors as school philosophy, the size of the school, the composition of the student body, the makeup of the local staff, the space and equipment at hand, and the available help from consultations play a role in shaping the innovation of the local schools. "Some innovations can be easily introduced and adapted with local variations, while others may not be as easily adaptable in different locations."[1]

Bhagia et al., (1990) in their book, 'Educational Administration in India and Other Developing Countries, p. 169' about Adaptability, Buch (1972) studied conditions promoting adaptability or innovativeness in Indian Schools. Her inquiry started with forty-nine factors suspected of influencing school adaptability. Most of the factors related to climatic dimension in the school were also taken up. By using the multiple correlation analysis, she found five variables influencing school-adaptability. The five variables are inter-school visitation, self-rated administrative ability, parent's involvement, professional meetings attended, and feeling of security.[2]

Tomasevski (2006) refers to adaptability as a "utopian" feature of the right to education. Adaptability is critical of traditional approaches and advocates greater results.[3]

2.5. Accountability

It can be seen from the foregoing pages that there were many studies regarding the administration of the Right to Education, but very few studies were conducted specifically on 'Accountability' in the administration of the right to education. The present study attempts to touch the aspect of accountability of the administration in the right to education. It also tries

1. Bhagia, N., Briggs, D., & Bhagia, S. (1990). *Educational administration in India and other developing countries: Challenges, tasks and training*. Commonwealth Publishers. p. 169.
2. *Ibid.*
3. Klees, S. J., & Thapliyal, N. (2007). *The right to education: The work of Katarina Tomasevski.* Comparative Education Review, 51(4), 497-510.

to suggest some necessary measures to increase the accountability of the administration in the right to education.

Wilcox (2000) says that inspection is a process of reform through change as a mechanism of accountability. Things like scheduling inspections, defining action plans, inspection processes, etc. affect the administrators involved in schools and they can be adaptable to change. However, the problem arises when it comes to implementing inspection properly.[1]

Pritchett et al., (2006) in their book talk about applying accountability criteria, there are three characteristics of an activity or function within an activity that influence the level at which accountability should be placed.

(a) **Discretionary:** Discretionary activities are those that require decisions to be made using individual judgments in a local context.

(b) **Transaction Intensity:** Transaction-intensive activities are those that require several repeated transactions at the local level.

(c) **Observability:** At what level can performance be based observed? If the activity is technically complicated. For this, technical evaluation, as well as local-level evaluation, is very important.[2]

According to **(Mishra, 2007)** about the accountability of the headmaster, the point here is that there are no poor schools. There are poor headmasters. The headmaster's personality plays an important role in determining the development of the school and children to a large extent.[3]

Dossing (2011) in their book talks about the accountability of educational administration and says accountability means holding individuals and organisations responsible for executing their powers properly. Dosing states that accountability includes capacity, participation, and integrity. Capacity means the capacity of the administrators for the work for which the administrators are appointed, as well as the ability for the participation of people from weaker sections. Participation can include location, time, public consultation, hearing, decisions of citizens committees or representatives of activities, etc. Integrity may include actions and practices consistent with ethical principles and standards.[4]

---

1. Wilcox, B. (2000). *Making school inspection visits more effective: The English experience.* UNESCO, International Institute for Educational Planning.
2. Pritchett, L., & Pande, V. (2006). *Making Primary Education Work for India's Rural Poor: A Proposal for Effective Decentralisation.* New Delhi: World Bank.
3. Mishra, R. C. (2007). *History of education administration.* APH Pub. p. 45.
4. Dossing, H. (2011). *Mapping transparency, accountability and integrity in primary education in South Africa.* Transparency International.

Edmondson (2012) says about accountability that, accountability works only with consistency, honesty, and intentions. Regular feedback is required to maintain consistency in accountability. Edmondson says about transparency that, honesty and transparency are synonyms in many ways, but transparency also suggests us to see through the aspects of who we are and what is within us.[1]

The New National Curriculum of UK, 2013 says in its recommendations that, in any type of school, whether it is government or private, it is very important for teachers to have the autonomy to decide how to teach children. Strong and clear accountability as well as a high level of autonomy is the most prevalent and effective education system worldwide. All schools should be accountable to parents, administrators, and the government. Having more and more data available increases accountability. Lord Bew believes that by publishing more and more data, parents and the public will be able to know about the achievements of the school.[2]

In a 2015 article, **The Hindu** reported that the Allahabad High Court had expressed frustration with the judicial system regarding the lack of oversight in managing government schools in Uttar Pradesh. The decisions were welcomed in several quarters, as a measure to increase accountability that would lead to improved teaching standards. We need to see that the biggest reason for the increase in private schools is the lack of access to government schools. The way, in which the population of the country has increased, the number of government schools in the rural areas of the country has not increased in the last two decades. Due to the apathy of government teachers and administration, the situation has continuously worsened. The most damaging aspect of the private schooling system is that private schools do not want to take responsibility for the moral growth and behaviour of the child.[3]

According to **John Porter,** 'Accountability is related to the guarantee of all students without distinction of caste, social status difference and the benefits of all the facilities of the school of economic level.'[4]

Similarly, **Peter Drucker** has accounted for the responsiveness of accountability to get results. All educational systems have any kind

1. Edmondson, R. (2012, July 2). *3 Keys to Effective Accountability*. https://ronedmondson.com/2012/07/3-keys-to-effective-accountability.html.
2. UK. (2013). *Primary assessment and accountability under the new national curriculum.* Department of Education, UK.
3. Setting standards for schools. (2016, July 13). The Hindu, 2016. Retrieved from https://www.thehindu.com/opinion/op-ed/setting-standards-for-schools/article7735243.ece
4. Addonizio, M., & Kearney, C. P. (2012). *Education reform and the limits of policy: Lessons from Michigan.* WE Upjohn Institute.

of accountability regardless of whether it is governmental or non-governmental. Accountability of all has been ensured to achieve the objectives of education so that all the components of the responsibility fulfil their responsibility with utmost dignity. All the components of education have been considered as a teacher's more important responsibility. The teacher is regarded as a nation-builder, a guide to society, and a culture nutritionist.[1]

2.5.1. Accountability in India Before Independence

Vedic Period: It was considered the responsibility of the guru in the Vedic period that he will give thought, contemplation, memory, and other mental actions to his students at the time of teaching, it was also the responsibility of the guru in that period that the conduct of education should be given not only book knowledge.

Middle Ages: Most of the time the Mughals occupied India in the Middle Ages. They emphasised religious education. The education system was decided according to the nature of the king. At that time, accountability of education could only be considered against the king.

British Period: At the beginning of the modern period, the education system is related to the rule of the British. Formal education institutions were established in this period. The main purpose of the education policy of the education and Education Principles of Lord Macaulay that Indians used to run their governance system. So, the question of the liability of teachers was not important.[2]

2.5.2. Accountability in India After Independence

The highest attention was given to the education sector after attaining independence. It attempted to bring the country's scattered education system under one formula. Under this, many commissions, committees, and education policies were constituted. e.g.:

1. Mudaliar Education Commission (1952-53)
2. Kothari Education Commission (1964-66)
3. National Education Policy (1968)
4. National Education Policy (1986) amended in 1992.

After attaining independence, the need for complete improvement in education was experienced and many commissions gave their suggestions

---

1. Drucker, P. F. (2004). *What makes an effective executive?* Harvard business review, 82(6).
2. Sinclair, P. (2014). *Basics in Education.* Text Book for B. Ed Course.

which all emphasised the responsibility of the teachers in different ways. The responsibilities of teachers are related to the job evaluation of teachers. The teacher defines responsibility or accountability in the word itself. The nature of the responsibilities of teachers in different periods remained different.

In the current scenario, the reciprocity of teachers' accountability is becoming more important. The direction is given to the entire society by education. It is the educationist who changes the direction.

According to the New Education Policy (1986), "There is an expression of responsibility, accountability by a worker to his work. This indicates the expected work done by the worker."[1] Accountability can be defined as the assessment of an individual's performance within the scope of their given responsibilities. This assessment can be carried out by any governing body or community. On the other hand, educational responsiveness refers to the ability to fulfil the educational and co-educational roles of a school with a strong sense of responsibility.[2]

The area of teacher accountability is very broad and serious; nevertheless, they consider themselves responsible for completing courses, preparing for exam preparation, evaluating answer points, making progress, etc. The ideal teacher is responsible for studying, keeping knowledge current, and evaluating educational activities. He should raise awareness of the study in the students, calm their inquiries, create a sense of co-existence, develop ethical values and national consciousness, create trends for social engagement, and enhance their morale. It is, therefore, the responsibility of the teachers to adapt themselves to changing education values, with new zeal and enthusiasm, and pave the way for future generations with their best educational capabilities because, in the 21st century, India has to become the world's leader in every field. This expectation of the country can only fulfil the active and intensive role of teachers in the education process. But together they must keep in mind the needs of the present century. Today information technology is spreading in the country. It has opened new doors of progress in every field, but the responsibilities of teachers for admission to them have increased.

In the current scenario, the connotation of teacher's responsiveness is becoming very important, because the perception is that educational achievement is not in line with society.

---

1. Government of India (1992). *National policy on education 1986*. Programme of action, 1992.
2. Raghavan, J. V. (1986). *Implementation of the New Education Policy-1986.* Indian Journal of Public Administration, 32(3), 521-534.

The value of accountability contexts lies in their purpose. Discussing one reference, the main objective of accountability is to maintain its quality. When the person emphasises the quality of work, then accountability works as an inspiration.

There may be many facets of teachers' accountability, such as guidance of students, loyalty to the work given by the principal, maintaining school discipline, initiative tendency, punctuality, honesty, business growth, maintenance and use of physical equipment, contribution to school growth and development, etc.

Increasing teacher accountability is an essential step as learning improves, according to the report, the attendance of teachers in primary and secondary schools was observed to be only 85%.[1] Improvement is needed to increase the attendance of the teachers in schools and the qualitative education of the students. The process of these reforms requires better assessment as well as more monitoring and support systems. Overall, the public school system needs to be improved by a better general management system.

The teacher should be prepared for three types of accountabilities:

(a) Product responsiveness: Be responsible for the achievement of the students,

(b) Process accountability: In the process, the teacher is accountable for his professional skills, knowledge, and organs,

(c) Experimental accountability: It involves all the programmes by which the teacher wants to make the teaching process more productive and effective.

1. Sahni, U. (2015). *Primary education in India: Progress and challenges.* The Brookings Institute. Retrieved from https://www.brookings.edu/opinions/primary-education-in-india-progress-and-challenges.

Research Methodology in Public Administration

Chapter - III

Research Methodology in Public Administration

3.1. Introduction

This chapter focuses on research concepts and methods relevant to an empirical study on the "Right to Education through the Lens of Public Administration". This study aims to know about the indicators like, availability of resources, affordability of resources, acceptability of teachers and administrators, adaptability of parents towards RTE, and how can the quality of the right to education be increased through accountability in administration.

3.2. Research Methodology in Social Sciences

Contemporary society is a scientific society. It analyzes related events and situations intellectually and logically to attain knowledge or suitable solutions to a problem. Along with society's development, man's attitude has developed to try to understand other activities of his society on scientific grounds.

Since man is a curious and contemplative animal, he wanders thinking. And it is constantly moving towards the detection of unknown facts. First, it tried to understand natural phenomena and then social events. It always tried to clarify the natural conditions and social complexities. It also tried to find out the truth of the knowledge gained. He tried to find the relation between works by using the scientific method to various events and created new principles. It has examined the veracity of the old principles from a new perspective.

Every research starts with a question or problem. It can be said without exaggeration that words such as "why," "what," "how," "when," and "who" form the essence of research. Its importance is indispensable in every research work.

Research is conducted to search for new facts or theories. In which careful examination, adequate observation, and architectural studies are done to obtain new knowledge. Research is a systematic scientific way of acquiring knowledge about events accessing the origins of those events and finding work-cause relationships.

It is thus clear that in research, the researcher studies deeply according to his curiosity. Whether it is natural conditions or social complexities based on his curiosity, it is the research to clarify the knowledge related to it and verify the knowledge gained, follow the old principles, and create new theories.

When any research is related to social life, social events, or social complexities, then it is called social research. In it, empirical facts are discovered for accurate knowledge. In this, the causes of social events are found based on inspection, testing, classification, and verification. In the field of social research, the initial step involves observing the fundamental aspects of a behaviour, issue, or occurrence to gain a comprehensive understanding of its overall characteristics. Subsequently, the focus shifts to uncovering the underlying causes of the problem. Social research places significant importance on using the scientific method to reveal and understand social phenomena.

P. V. Young says that we can define social research as a scientific undertaking governing logical and systematic methods of discovering new or old facts, analyzing their interrelationships, causal explanations, sequence, and natural laws, etc."[1]

It is thus clear that social research is such a method of discovery in which any event, practice, social life, or problem in the context of social situation an attempt is made to understand social reality by using the scientific method.

3.3. Research Methodology in Public Administration

Research in the field of public administration has undergone substantial evolution in recent years. These developments encompass changes in research methodologies, the interdisciplinary nature of theories applied, and the evolving scope of research inquiries. Moreover, there is a noticeable trend in public-sector values shifting from a focus on efficiency and effectiveness to emphasising equity. According to Mele & Belardinelli

1. Slesinger, D., & Stephenson, M. (1930). *The Encyclopaedia of Social Sciences.* Vol. IX. MacMillan.

(2019), in public administration, the increasing adoption of methodological pluralism, often referred to as a mixed-methods approach, is highly significant. We perceive opportunities within public administration research to make meaningful and recognizable contributions toward solving many of the societal challenges we currently encounter.[1]

Walmsley (1996) believes that public administration is not just a social science type subject but should be seen as an 'applied interdisciplinary field'. Wessels, Paw, and Thani (2009) believe that public administration can be classified as a human science, social management, and administrative science.

Pauw (1995) has identified seven different scientific disciplines under human science, in which he has considered skills and empirical social science methods in public administration as the most important.

Public administration is characterised by a multidisciplinary nature. This means that public administration draws upon knowledge and methodologies from various fields of study, not limited to a single discipline. Specifically, the disciplines such as empirical social sciences play a significant role in public administration. It implies that these disciplines contribute prominently to shaping and understanding public administration as described within the book's context.

Public administration has a multi-disciplinary nature and the disciplines and methods of the empirical social sciences, among others, feature very prominently within it.[2]

This reflection will specifically reflect on the variety of research methods applicable to public administration as a human science, suggesting a focused exploration of the different research methods that can be used within the realm of public administration, considering it as a field belonging to the humanities or social sciences.

Research in public administration as:

(a) **Focus on research methods**: The phrase "variety of research methods" indicates that the reflection will discuss different approaches, techniques, and methodologies that researchers can employ when studying topics related to public administration.

---

1. McDonald III, B. D., Hall, J. L., O'Flynn, J., & van Thiel, S. (2022). The future of public administration research: An editor's perspective. *Public Administration, 100*(1), 59-71.
2. Wessels, J. S., Pauw, J. C., & Thani, X. C. (Eds.). (2014). *Reflective Public Administration: context, knowledge, and methods*. Unisa Press.

(b) **Applicability to public administration**: It emphasises that the discussion is specifically tailored to public administration, highlighting that this field has distinct characteristics and requirements that influence the choice of research methods.

(c) **Viewing public administration as a human science**: By describing public administration as a "human science," the sentence positions it within the broader category of disciplines that study human behaviour, societies, and institutions. This implies an emphasis on understanding the complexities of human interactions, decision-making processes, and organisational dynamics within the context of administrative systems.

(d) **Reflective nature**: The use of "reflection" indicates that the discussion will involve critical examination and analysis, possibly weighing the strengths, limitations, and appropriateness of various research methods within the specific context of public administration.

In summary, it indicates a deliberate examination of how different research methods can be utilised within public administration, emphasising its human science aspect and suggesting an evaluative or contemplative approach to understanding and applying these methods effectively.

3.4. Research Methodology

After initial knowledge about the research topic, the researcher creates a theory in his mind, which he imagines may be the basis of his research. A researcher does not follow such a hypothetical conclusion as the ultimate, but he tries to prove his authenticity by his experience and real facts.

Any method is a scientific method that a non-biased scholar uses to study a subject. **Stuart Chase** also believes that "Science goes with the method, not with the content."

Therefore, the scientific method is a strong basis to replace any subject as science. Every scientific study is related to a complete methodology or procedure. From the beginning of the research work to the generalisation, the research journey has to go through many processes. Based on these processes an interpretation or serialisation takes place in the scientific method. Please remember the following guidelines for this procedure, taking into account the rigorous standards and protocols of scientific research.

This research is done by certain steps or by a certain method, which includes the following steps of research:

1. Formulation of the problem or selection of the problem
2. Determination of study objectives
3. Review of Literature
4. Formulation of Hypothesis
5. Research Design
6. Collection of Data
7. Analysis of Data
8. Generalisation and Interpretation
9. Preparation of the Report

Research done by serialisation of these various stages is called research method and the science in which it is studied is called research methodology.

In this way, research done by the scientific methods stages related to the changes in the social system is called social research. About social events or problems in research compile the certified and empirical facts through scientific methods and instruments like observation, interview, schedule, questionnaire, etc. The systematic process of creating new principles or rules through organising, categorising, studying, and making broad conclusions is known as research methodology.

For **Hall and Hall (1996)**, methodology should be seen as the philosophy or the general principles on which research is pursued.

According to **Williams (2007)**, researchers usually answer research questions requiring numerical data, choosing a quantitative approach; a qualitative approach is required for text data research questions, and research questions requiring both numerical and text returns require a mixed method approach.[1]

3.5. Combination of both Quantitative and Qualitative Approaches

In this study, research has been done with qualitative and quantitative methods. The objectives for this study (in chapter one) clearly show that this research intended to examine the main constituents of access to primary education, to develop suitable indicators of availability, affordability, acceptability, and adaptability, to identify the indicators

1. Williams, C. (2007). *Research methods*. Journal of Business & Economics Research (JBER), 5(3).

(among 4 A's) which are responsible for low access in the Varanasi of Uttar Pradesh and to identify the possibilities of an accountable educational administration.

3.5.1. Quantitative

A quantitative survey is interested in presenting data related to a topic in a statistical form. Whenever surveys are conducted to study subjects like percentage of literacy, per capita income or balance of income-expenditure, female-male ratio, and unemployment rate, these are called quantitative surveys. In surveys, the findings are typically shown as percentages or ratios through the use of statistical methods.

It is strongly believed that the results of this study would aid in understanding the state of education in the city of Varanasi. Quantitative data and statistical analysis would also help in testing some hypotheses and increase the validity of the findings from this study.

3.5.2. Qualitative

When a survey is related to a qualitative subject or event, it is called a qualitative survey. The purpose of such surveys is to study the attitude of a particular group, the impact of social values, ideas and limits of social change, etc. This implies that qualitative surveys are related to knowing psychological characteristics and through this, information is received about the good or bad of a particular event or a particular tendency.

In this study, there was a need for the researcher to dig deep to get a complete understanding of the situation from the perspective of the parents, teachers, and administrators concerning the right to education. Making statistical conclusions could not suffice in unveiling the picture of primary education in Varanasi city from different perspectives. In this study, the author tried to understand whether there was any kind of collaborative and cooperative relationship between the parents and the teachers and administrators in the school management committee. Special focus was stressed on the challenges of how to improve the accountability in the right to education.

3.6. Case Study Approach

In the social sciences, a case study is a descriptive, exploratory, or explanatory analysis of an individual, group, or event. An exploratory case study is used to find underlying theories; case studies may be prospective or retrospective.

About case studies, **Thomas (2011)** says that a case study is widely studied in one or several ways that include analysis of individuals, decisions, periods, events, projects, policies, institutions, or other systems.[1]

Creswell (1998) considered a case study to be a system of in-depth data collection and study from time to time.[2]

The purpose of this research is exploratory. This type of research is typically qualitative, allowing for the exploration and testing of hypotheses. The assumption is that the researcher has little or no knowledge about the problem or situation; he is also unfamiliar with the structure he is studying.

In exploratory research, the case study method is its basic design, because a case study is an exploration of one or several cases.[3] In this research, the case studied was the role of administration in the right to education in the city of Varanasi. In this type of research structure, prior study of related literature is mandatory, thereafter, people related to the problem should be contacted, in which special attention should be focused on the problem from a social perspective.

3.7. Research Design

In this study, qualitative data was used in the study area to create a better picture of the right to education as well as to enrich the details found by quantitative data. It includes aspects of phenomenological study design of research to guide qualitative data collection and analysis.

Since the researcher was interested in finding out the attitudes, beliefs, and perceptions of the parents, teachers, and administrators regarding the right to education, phenomenology was a paramount component of this research design. Therefore, knowledge would be constructed from the researcher's interpretation of the respondents' interpretations.[4]

This study is skewed toward qualitative research, experimentation may not be appropriate. The current investigation employed a combination of interviews, observations, and questionnaires as research tools, aiming to provide a comprehensive and multifaceted approach to data collection and analysis.

3.8. Study Area

Purposively selected the area of Varanasi Municipal Corporation

1. Gary, T. (2011). *How to do your case study: A guide for students and researchers.* Thousand Oaks, CA: Sage Publications.
2. Creswell, J. W. (1998). *Qualitative research and research design: Choosing among five traditions.* London: Thousand Oaks, CA: Sage Publications.
3. *Ibid.*
4. Bryman, A. (2012). *Social research methods.* OUP Oxford.

(VMC) of Varanasi is located in the eastern region of Uttar Pradesh and is financially a wealthy area. The Varanasi district lies between 25° 20' north latitude and 83° 00' east longitude.[1] The city of Varanasi is surrounded by the holy Ganges River. Varanasi is the oldest city in the world. Presently there are 90 wards under the Varanasi Municipal Corporation and the total area under it is 79.79 Sq. /Km. Currently, Varanasi has also been included in the Smart City Project. According to the 2011 census, the total population of Varanasi district is about 3682194. In terms of population, Varanasi ranks 18th in the state of Uttar Pradesh. The population density of Varanasi district is about 2395 persons per square kilometer which is more than the state average of 829 persons per sq. km. (District Statistical Handbook, 2011).

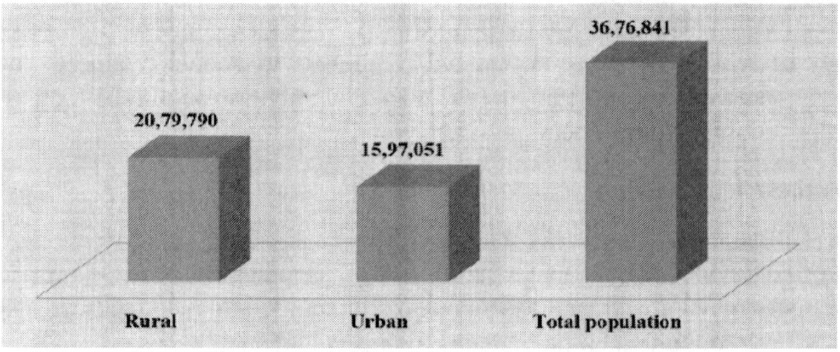

Source: District Statistical Handbook, 2011.

Figure 3.1: Demographic Profile of Varanasi.

3.9. Sample Design

In simple terms, it is selected from the whole of the population. In other words, the sample is determined based on the process of knowledge, the process of which moves from small to large. If we want to get information about the whole population, then through the process of the sample, we can get information by examining only a part of the population. Technically selected various items constitute a sample, all techniques and procedures to use their selection are called sample design and the survey conducted with the help of a sample is called a sample survey. The more the selection of the sample is independent of personal bias, the more scientific is expected in the study. Therefore, a proper model is completely independent of individual bias.[2]

1. Latitude and Longitude of Uttar Pradesh, (2011). Map of India, 2011. Retrieved from https://www.mapsofindia.com/lat_long/uttarpradesh/
2. Kothari, C. R. (2004). *Research methodology: Methods and techniques*. New Age International.

The size of a sample is determined by the style of research.[1] In this study, which is a combination of quantitative and qualitative techniques, current research is based on purposive sampling. In this, the sample is chosen for a specific purpose, this is why it is called objective, decision-related, or judgemental sampling. In purposive sampling, the researcher already knows the units to be inserted or omitted. In this, the nature and idea of the researcher is more important.

According to **Jahoda et al. (1955)**, there is a fundamental assumption that a person with appropriate skills and appropriate judgment as a sample can select cases which can be called purposive sampling.[2]

3.9.1. Population

This book aims to conduct a study of the population of Varanasi Municipal Corporation (VMC) which is 1,597,051 (Census, 2011).

3.9.2. Sample Unit

Anything that forms the basis of choosing your sample is called a sample unit. The sample unit of this study is the primary schools of Varanasi. The universe of this study is parents of the children along with teachers and administrators related to the right to education in Varanasi city.

3.9.3. Sample Size

Sample size determination is a problematic issue. And finding a representative sample size is even more problematic. For this study too, keeping in mind the various concerns, 351 respondents i.e. 117 parents and 234 teachers and administrators have been chosen for data collection. These respondents have been selected based on the Taro Yamane Formula as a researcher was seriously concerned with collecting representative samples from different primary schools as there have been wide variations among the schools in terms of government and private status.

3.9.4. Precision Level

In the present research, the urban area has been studied, i.e. total number of government and private primary schools in the urban area of Varanasi is 166 after reducing 1204 primary schools in the rural area of Varanasi from a total of 1370 primary schools of Varanasi district. In the present study,

---

1. Cohen, L., Manion, L., & Morrison, K. (2013). *Research methods in education.* Routledge.
2. Jahoda, M., & Barnitz, E. (1955). *The nature of evaluation.* International Social Science Bulletin, 7(3), 1-13.

a total of 351 respondents comprising 117 parents, 117 teachers, and 117 administrators were interviewed through the interview schedule.

Yamane (1967) suggested a simplified formula for calculating the size of a population.[1] According to him, for a 95% confidence level and p = 0.5, the size of the sample should be:

$$n = N/\ \{1 + N\,(e)^2\}$$

{Where, Population Size (N) and Level of Precision (e)}

$$n = 166/\ \{1+166(.05)^2\} = 117 \text{ Approx.}$$

3.9.5. Sampling Methods and Procedure

For selecting samples from the population, the cluster random sampling method was employed first as it has not been feasible for the researcher to conduct household surveys on the whole area and population of the city. Wards under the Varanasi Municipal Corporation were taken into consideration for the correct selection of samples. And 40 out of 90 wards have been selected randomly by writing the names of all 90 wards on small pieces of paper. The 40 wards that were selected: 3-Lahartara, 4-Shivpurva, 5-Hukulganj, 7-Naibasti, 8-Rajghat, 9-Saraisurjan, 10-Tarna, 11-Nagwa, 13-Newada, 14-Nawabganj, 15-Sikraul, 16-Pandeypur, 17-Narayanpur, 18-Nadesar, 19-Tulsipur, 21-Chaukaghat, 22-Shivpur, 26-Paharia, 27-Birdopur, 29-Sundarpur, 31-Naria, 32-Sigra, 33-Sarnath, 34-Khazuri, 35-Ramrepur, 37-Jagatganj, 40-Khojwa, 42-Nawapura, 43-Konia, 44-Kameshwar Mahadev, 45-Bhelupur, 52-Kajipura, 54-Katuapura, 55-Bhadaini, 58-Dhupchandi, 62-Luxa, 68-Shivala, 71-Bangalitola, 81-Dashashwamedh, 85-Kaalbhairav. Once wards have been selected randomly, 8-9 respondents from each ward i.e. 351 respondents have been

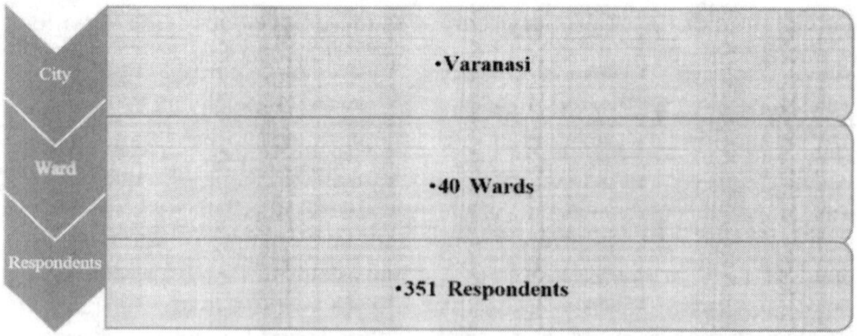

Figure 3.2: Sample Selection Process.

1. Yamane, T. (1967). *Problems to accompany "Statistics, an introductory analysis"*. Harper & Row.

surveyed based on convenience sampling to have the sample drawn from a dispersed area, to avoid getting the sample from one place.

Many people were not willing to give the information for the research interview schedule. Some refused out rightly, while others made excuses for paucity of time. Some questioned the utility of the study; others thought it was of no use. This constraint also justifies the use of convenience sampling in primary school surveys.

3.10. Data Collection Methods

The method of collection of data should be well understood and carefully selected by the researcher so that the quality of research remains. It also depends on the need and objectives of research, and which sources are necessary for the data. The more reliable and accessible the sources of data collection are the more success will be achieved in collecting the data. This study aims to focus on both qualitative and quantitative methods.

3.10.1. Pilot Survey

Pilot testing of various close-ended and open-ended questions was done through an interview schedule before the primary survey was conducted in Varanasi. During this, an effort was made to know the views of various parents of the 6-14-year-old children, teachers, and administrators of the primary schools. During the pilot survey, the researcher found that various respondents were hesitant and faced difficulties in answering many questions. And later schedule was modified accordingly. Subsequently, two types of interview schedules consisting of Likert Scale-type questions were prepared i.e., first, for the parents and second, for the teachers and administrators. After that, the primary survey was conducted in different urban and semi-urban areas of Varanasi city.

3.10.2. Survey

When the researcher collects the data by contacting the respondents of their study area or the whole, it is called the primary source of data collection.

Data were collected from the respondents using the schedules for the assessment of availability, affordability, acceptability (attitude of teachers and administrators), adaptability (response of receivers), accountability of educational administration, and so on. A convenience sampling-based primary school survey of 351 respondents (i.e. 117 parents and 234 teachers and administrators) was conducted in the 40 wards of the city.

Respondent's perceptions about the existing primary education system were rated on an ordinal scale from 1 to 5, with 1 being - Not satisfied at all and 5 - Extremely satisfied. Scores and analyses were conducted with SPSS.

3.10.3. Observation

It is one of the most important sources of collecting data. For the collection of data, it is very important to have a consciousness of observation in the researcher, because the researcher collects information using various methods. In this, the researcher himself goes to the study area and studies related events and behaviours. Researchers can do this work by taking part in events and programmes of related study areas or as viewers. The researcher includes facts that are worthy of observation and which can be kept in writing.

Through the observation method, the information is directly observed by the investigator without getting answers from the respondents.[1] The researcher needs to use observation to increase information about the event. The observation technique has the advantage that it is flexible and can provide a naturally accurate description of events.

In this study researcher has undertaken non-participant and unstructured observation during visits to the field while collecting survey data and conducting interviews. This researcher observed first-hand, the situations of primary and so on.

In this regard, Cohen and others contend that it is more tenable to argue that participant observation is the most personally demanding and analytically difficult method of social research to undertake.

3.10.4. Interviewing

Through this, the researcher collects the information by establishing direct contact with the respondents himself. Because the respondents have a close relationship with local problems and also know other sources related to the problem, hence, reliable and beneficial information can be obtained from them at a personal level, through conversation.

It is therefore meant to enable the collection of data that are related to the research questions and overall research problem.[2] In addition, interview in research has multiple forms which may be structured or unstructured, individual or group interviews.

1. Kothari, C. R. (2004). *Research methodology: Methods and techniques*. New Age International.
2. Leedy, P. D., & Ormrod, J. E. (2013). *Practical research: Planning and design*. Boston, MA: Merrill.

3.11. Data Collection Instruments

3.11.1. Schedule

Through this, the researcher goes to the respondents and fills in the answers to the questions related to the problem or topic. Questions and blank tables are given in the schedule. The purpose of the schedule is to get subjectivity in research by getting answers from respondents. The schedule is beneficial for research. In this, the questions cannot be asked by twisting or distorting, the order of questions remains the same. Because the questions are in written form, the researcher does not necessarily have to memorise them. The information received by the schedule is very useful as it is unbiased. The schedule includes open-ended questions and close-ended questions.

Usually, the response to an open question can be long. Open-ended questions are usually asked to elicit the opinions and thoughts of the respondents. They need thinking and reflection; the answer to an open question is often descriptive and explanatory. Open-ended questions usually begin with words like how, why, what, and description.

A closed question can be answered in one word or short phrase. Sometimes, a closed question is also defined as a question that can be answered in a yes or no.

In this study researcher has collected data using interview schedules which the researcher has filled with information collected from respondents during the field survey.

3.11.2. Data

Secondary sources of data are those sources from which information received is not of the first level. It is researched by someone else first. The material from secondary sources is often published or unpublished in which the researcher receives other useful information.

Secondary data sources are listed below:

1. Report Cards published by of National University of Educational Planning and Administration (NUEPA).
2. Publish work of the Department of School Education and Literacy, Ministry of Human Resource Development, Government of India.
3. Reports of Programme for International Student Assessment (PISA).
4. Annual Status of Education Report (ASER) by Pratham.

5. EFA Global Monitoring Report by UNESCO.
6. School Education Quality Index (SEQI).
7. Reports related to Varanasi City, etc.
8. Books, academic journals, articles, websites, and newspaper reports concerning the administration of primary education.

3.12. Data Analysis

After collecting the data, the task of analyzing them is very important. The success of any social research depends only on how the data collected is analyzed. After the collection of data and facts, the social scientist focuses all his attention on their analysis and interpretation. That is, a researcher analyzes and interprets facts by placing them in a systematic order through process; only then social studies have the merit of scientism.

The analysis of data that were meant to address the research questions presented in chapter one of this book, focuses on the different indicators of primary education and so on. Inferences have been drawn based on the analysis of data. The present study analyzed the complete data with the help of frequency tables and cross-tabulation.

3.13. Limitations of the Study

The author faced various types of difficulties during the collection of facts. Some were situational and a few were self-imposed. Firstly, the findings of the study are limited to the study area of Varanasi city. This study is based on only 351 respondents covering 40 wards, so the findings of this study may not be universally generalised. Secondly, this study is confined to respondents i.e. parents, teachers, and administrators only; senior-level officials were kept outside the purview of the study. Different primary education issues have been discussed and debated with officials only informally to enrich the understanding of primary education. Thirdly, the study is limited to urban and semi-urban areas of the Varanasi district. Fourthly, male respondents were surveyed more than females as parents of children did not let them respond to the survey except for a few cases. Fifthly, the findings of the study are based on responses given by the parents, teachers, and administrators of primary education.

3.14. Conclusion

The two major approaches to research methodology in social science, namely quantitative research and qualitative research have been analyzed in this chapter. Qualitative research, in general, focuses on how individuals and groups perceive and understand their social world and construct meaning from their experiences. The data collection methods that have been analyzed in the chapter are the primary school survey, interviewing, and observation. Data was collected using a schedule that was supplemented and corroborated with unstructured observation and interviews as well.

Right to Education: A Global Perspective

Chapter - IV

Right to Education: A Global Perspective

4.1. Right to Education in the Global Scenario

Education has been globally recognised as a fundamental human right and people through education or with access to education can develop skills, abilities, and confidence to secure other rights.[1]

Article 26 (1) of the Universal Declaration of Human Rights (UDHR), states that "Everyone has the right to education. Primary education will be necessary and free at least in the elementary and fundamental stages."[2]

The International Covenant on Economic, Social, and Cultural Rights (ICESCR) adopted by the United Nations in 1966 also recognised the importance of the right to education and gave its approval and recognition.

In directing children's education, the fundamental role of their parents is recognised under Article 18(4) of ICCPR.[3]

Keeping in view the importance and inevitability of education, human development has adopted it as a basic human right globally and expressed in letter 26 of the Universal Declaration of Human Rights (1948). Education was accepted as a major basic right in the Conference on Child Rights in 1989, Rights of children were announced on December 20, 1989, by the United Nations General Assembly. This declaration has 54 articles.

1. Schools in Arunachal Pradesh, (2020). In Schools, 2020. Retrieved from https://www.inschools.in/state/Arunachal-Pradesh.html
2. Delphine Dorsi. (2014, December 10). *The Right to Education: a Daily Challenge.* https://www.right-to-education.org/blog/right-education-daily-challenge.
3. International Covenant on Civil and Political Rights, (2020). United Nations Human Rights, 2020. Retrieved from https://www.ohchr.org/en/professionalinterest/pages/ccpr.aspx

According to Article 28, all countries involved in the agreement recognise the rights of children's education, followed by the World Child Summit held in New York in 1990, and by the year 2000, the emphasis was on achieving the goal of education for all.[1]

On the other hand, a world-class education seminar was held in Jomtien City, Thailand.[2] About 1500 delegates from 155 countries of the world, including experts from the World Bank, UNESCO, and United Nations Development Programme (UNDP), participated in this conference. In this seminar, a consensus was made to provide education to all by the year 2000. Functional points were set up by the conference, i.e., to make primary education more friendly, to provide equal opportunities to all, broaden the tools and work area, emphasise learning, educate in the educational environment, mobilisation of resources, develop a policy of help/cooperation/coordination, and strengthening international unity. An action plan was prepared for achieving desired goals at the national level for this. This work plan, focused on special education was given to girls' education and facilities for the education of the children of deprived sections, improvement in education level, community involvement, and the support of educational organisations.

4.1.1. Dakar World Education Conference: Education for all

With the observation of the Jamaican World Education Conference 1990, World Education Conference, 2000 was organised at the international level in Dakar, Senegal (South Africa). All countries have pledged to make universal, free, compulsory, and quality education available by the year 2015.[3] The 6 goals mentioned in the declaration of the Dakar Conference are as follows:

1. Widening and promotion of comprehensive child care and education programmes, especially for the most vulnerable and poor children of disadvantaged sections,
2. To ensure the free, complete, and excellent quality compulsory primary education to all children, especially girls, living in different conditions and for minority children by 2015,

---

1. History of child rights, (2020). Unicef, for every child, 2020. Retrieved from https://www.unicef.org/child-rights-convention/history-child-rights
2. Haggis, S. M. (1991). *Education for All: Purpose and Context.* World Conference on Education for All (Jomtien, Thailand, March 5-9, 1990). Monograph I. Roundtable Themes I. Unesco Press, 7, place de Fontenoy, 75700 Paris, France.
3. Harsch, E. (2000). *Dakar summit urges renewed global drive to achieve basic education for all.* Africa Recovery, 14(2), 14-18.

3. To ensure the fulfillment of the learning needs of all boys and girls and adults through appropriate learning and life skill-related programmws and accessibility in the same manner,
4. By the year 2005, 50 percent improvement in adult literacy levels through access to basic and continuing education for all adults, especially women,[1]
5. To eliminate gender inequality in primary and secondary education by the year 2015,
6. To improve the quality of education and to ensure their excellence.

4.1.2. Education for Sustainable Development (ESD)

Through education, teachers and learners need to achieve the goal of sustainable development by reflecting critically on their communities. A holistic understanding of three major areas such as society, environment, and economy can be developed with culture for sustainable development.[2]

4.1.3. United Nations Millennium Declaration, 2000

The following are some points related to education in the Millennium Declaration:

1. To make people aware that, education is a sustainable way of life.
2. Ensuring that schools, colleges, universities, and other modes of learning are concerned is an idea of sustainable development.
3. People can learn from new experiences and activities in different parts of the world, ensuring that organisations and governments around the world work together.[3]

4.1.4. Decentralisation of Educational Administration in the World

Education Deconcentration: Education Deconcentration is a process when the Union Ministry of Education, assigns some of its responsibilities to the regional or local offices. But these offices are only part of the central administration. In **Germany**, the state is the primary decision-maker of primary and secondary schools. The state makes its own rules regarding the maximum number of students for each class. However, the final decision

---

1. Barakat, B. (2016). '*Improving adult literacy without improving the literacy of adults?* A cross-national cohort analysis. World Development, 87, 242-257.
2. Purvis, B., Mao, Y., & Robinson, D. (2019). *Three pillars of sustainability: in search of conceptual origins.* Sustainability science, 14(3), 681-695.
3. Assembly, U. G. (2000). *United Nations Millennium Declaration.* Resolution adopted by the General Assembly 55/2, 8 September.

for extra school in a school is taken by the local educational administration. And a school can apply to the further class.

Education Devolution: Educational devolution is the process when the central government assigns its responsibilities to a local independent and elected government, such as a state, province, or local authority. Such educational decentralisation can be seen in **Belgium** and **Spain**, where the educational administration is under the Belgian Language Communities and the Spanish Autonomous Communities respectively.

Education Delegation: Delegation means that the government hands over some decision-making powers to a local school through a tier, but to fulfill its decision-making is related to this tier of the government. For example, under the **Danish** primary school system, some municipalities have assigned their responsibility of decision-making to the concerned school, but Danish municipalities can reclaim their powers at any time.[1]

4.1.5. No Child Left Behind (NCLB) Act of America, 2001

Accountability in the United States has been considered a central theme under state policies for school reform. In the US, the No Child Left Behind (NCLB) Act of 2001, including accountability standards for schools, districts, and states, also ensures that design related to state testing requirements of education reform will be given importance.[2]

4.2. Administration of Primary Education in India Before Independence

4.2.1. Indian Primary Education in Ancient Times (600 B.C.)

According to Dr. A. S. Altekar, there was no provision of elementary education before 400 B.C. in ancient India. In ancient times, education was given at home only. The family was the center of education. Later, education was started in Gurukul. In primary education, the child was taught to pronounce and speak the first Vedanta. After memorising the mantras, they were taught to read and write. Women in this age had the right to education like men. There was also a system of co-education. Education was free; the entrance and study period at the age of 5 was up to 6 years.

In the Vedic Period, a strong system of primary education was made. This education was started in 'Vidyarambh Sanskar' for 5 years and the children of all castes could get the education. This education was under the control of the Brahmins and it was done in the ashram and Gurukulas

1. Werner, J. (2009). *Public administration in the education sector: boon or bane for Western Europe?* International Public Management Review, 10(2), 1-22.
2. Act, N. C. L. B. (2002). *No child left behind act of 2001.* Publ. L, 107-110.

beyond the family perimeter. The education system was dominated by religious institutions. This period of primary education is called the Golden Age. Because at this time elementary education was free and open to everyone.[1]

4.2.2. Primary Education in the Buddhist Period (500 B.C. to 1200 A.D.)

Buddhist education was similar to the Vedic period. But the differences in the beliefs of that era had come. Education in the Buddhist period was religion-oriented. It was divided into two levels, respectively religious education and higher education. The doors of Buddhist education were open to all religions, sections, and castes, but the adoption of Buddhism was compulsory. According to the Chinese traveller Hiuen Tsang who came to India in the seventh century, the age of initiating primary education was 6 years.[2]

The Chinese traveler Hiuen Stang has described the curriculum of elementary education that the child had to read the childhood book, Siddhirastu in the first 6 months. After 16 months, the child was given education in 5 disciplines - words, pedagogy, spirituality, crafts, and position.[3]

4.2.3. Primary Education in the Medieval Period (1200 A.D. to 1700 A.D.)

In this age, the main objective of education dissemination was to spread Islam and Muslim culture. Early education was started in 4 years, 4 months, 4 days at Makdab and higher education was given in Madarsas. Education was free, female education was not more prevalent. In the Muslim era, the emphasis was given to both professional education and discipline in both Hindus and Muslims. The main drawback of this education system was that special education was not given to the education of the masses. Education was limited to only the upper class. The royal house of the upper class was arranged for the education of women.[4]

4.2.4. Primary education in the British Period (1700 A.D. to 1947 A.D.)

Shortly after the arrival of European merchants in India, Christian missionaries entered the country. The main purpose of the missionaries

1. Altekar, A. S. (2009). *Education in ancient India.* Gyan Publishing House.
2. Pandya, D. R. N. (2014). *Indian education system: a historical journey.* Education, 3(3).
3. Aggarwal, J. C. (2007). *Development of education system in India.* Shipra.
4. *Ibid.*

was to make Indians a follower of their religion. They supported education for the promotion of his religion and established educational institutions at different places and they started the work of imparting education in the Western way. For this reason, missionaries are considered to be the promoters of modern education in India.[1]

The names of Raja Ram Mohan Roy, Ishwar Chandra Vidyasagar, Swami Dayanand Saraswati, etc. are notable, with their efforts, many elementary schools were established in India and education spread. The origins of modern education are attributed to the missionaries of British rule. In this era, the Filtration Theory of Education, Wood's Manifesto, the Indian Education Commission, the Hunter Commission, the Indian University Commission, the Hartog Committee, Basic Education, and the Sargent Report have special significance.[2]

4.2.5. Macaulay's Statement (1835)

The description paper of Lord Macaulay occupies an important place in the field of modern Indian education. In the words of Macaulay, In India, education was to create such people who are Indian in colour, but in English, in the way of worship, conversation, contemplation, thinking, and ideas.

Thus, the early education policy of the Britishers came to light that by educating the elite class of society through English, the concept of reaching the lower classes of society was achieved by scrutinising education. This concept is known in the field of Indian education as the 'downstream fusion principles'.[3]

4.2.6. Wood's Manifesto (1854)

He tried to give uniformity by understanding the diversity of Indian education. He implemented the scheme of order for educational institutions across the country. In this order letter, the local elementary schools were asked to encourage by granting them. In the letter of order, it was expressed that the oriental literature and indigenous languages should be encouraged. Books should be made in native languages and books of Western science and literature should be translated into Indian languages.[4]

1. Ring, T., & Salkin, R. M. (1996). *International dictionary of historic places.* Fitzroy Dearborn Publishers.
2. Sarkar, S. (1989). *Modern India 1885–1947.* Springer.
3. Thirumalai, M. S. (2003). *Lord Macaulay: The man who started it all, and his Minute.* Language in India, 3(4).
4. Jayapalan, N. (2005). *History of education in India.* Atlantic Publishers & Distributors.

4.2.7. Hunter Commission (Indian Education Commission) (1882)

The Hunter Commission is also known as the Indian Education Commission. This Commission was constituted only to consider primary education and its problems but it also suggested in the fields of secondary education, higher education, women's education, and modern education.[1]

4.2.8. Lord Curzon: A qualitative increase in education (1899)

In the second half of the nineteenth century, Indian masses were not satisfied with the education system of the Hunter Commission. They believed that only a few people can get Western education through English and the education of the people is being ignored. As a result, Indian culture is being lost. Lord Curzon came to India in 1899 as Viceroy. Curzon's impression was that by improving education, the administration can be improved. He raised the slogan of qualitative growth in education. He believed that primary education should be given more attention and its quality should be spread to provide education to the people. At the same time, he also increased the unpredictable amount of money spent on education.[2]

4.2.9. The Contribution of Gopal Krishna Gokhale (1910-1911)

Gopal Krishna Gokhale was extremely unhappy with the miserable situation of primary education in India. From 1910 to 1913, he worked tirelessly to make primary education compulsory and free. Gopal Krishna Gokhale presented a bill before the Government on March 10, 1911, in which primary education was made mandatory. The Central Government has not accepted this bill. But by getting inspiration from it, the Compulsory Education Act was made in many provinces. According to the Government proposals and suggestions of 1913, the number of primary schools increased but despite all these efforts, the progress of primary education remained satisfactory from 1905 to 1921.[3]

4.2.10. Hartog Committee (1927-1929)

The Hartog Committee acknowledged that although primary education is spreading, its progress is not satisfactory. He put special emphasis on reinforcement in place of the spread of schools. The idea of the committee was that the spread in the field of education was losing quality and the

---

1. Sharma, Y. K. (2001). *History and problems of education* (Vol. 1). Kanishka Publishers.
2. Bhattacharya, S. (1955, January). *The Men Who Ruled India, 1899—1901 (A sketch by Lord Curzon): In Proceedings of the Indian History Congress* (Vol. 18, pp. 209-216). Indian History Congress.
3. Mondal, A. (2017). *Free and Compulsory Primary Education in India under the British Raj: A Tale of an Unfulfilled Dream.* SAGE Open, 7(3), 2158244017727037.

urgent demand of time was to upgrade the quality and not to increase the quantitative. In the progress of primary education, he discussed two main obstacles, i.e., Wastage and Barriers. Hartog Committee gave several suggestions for the eradication of these problems, i.e., the Liberal curriculum of primary education, a trained teacher, priority of quality, the establishment of rural schools, and compulsory primary education.[1]

4.2.11. Wardha Education Conference (1937)

Mahatma Gandhi presented a new scheme for basic education before the present persons and said that the country's current education system could not meet the country's requirements in any way. Whatever the benefit of this education, the main class of the country becomes deprived. Therefore, the primary education course is at least seven years by which knowledge can be given to the matriculation[2]. But in this place, a good industry should be added to the place of English so that the cost can be paid. The government must procure the things they have made at the price fixed by the state.

4.2.12. Basic Education or 'Nai Talim' (1937)

Mahatma Gandhi described the 'Nai Talim' scheme in the year 1937 in his newspaper 'Harijan' with a well-crafted educational approach. It is a well-developed philosophy based on the experiments of Mahatma Gandhi from the year 1904 during his stay in South Africa along with Sabarmati (Gujarat) and Sewagram (Maharashtra) in India. It was an approach to the whole personality based on the development of body, mind, and soul which can be seen as basically four principles, such as; (i) Handicraft work along with education in the mother tongue, (ii) Work should be linked with the most useful local vocational needs, (iii) Learning must be linked with vocational functions, and (iv) Work should be productive needed for living and socially useful.[3]

4.2.13. Sargent Education Scheme (1944)

For primary education, the Sargent Report has accepted the basic education plan after some changes.[4] He has included primary and middle-

1. Maheshwari, V. K. (2012). *Evolution of Educational System in India.* Retrieved from http://www.vkmaheshwari.com/WP/?p=528
2. Wardha Scheme of Basic Education (1937). NeoStencil, 2019. Retrieved from https://neostencil.com/upsc-modern-history-wardha-scheme-basic-education-1937
3. Takwale, R., Sawant, V., & Deshmukh, M. N. (2010). *NaiTalim and Gandhian Approaches to Development*. North-South Dialogues.
4. The Sargent Report: Objects, Criticism and Defects: Education. (2016, August 30). Your article library, 2019. Retrieved from http://www.yourarticlelibrary.com/education/the-sargent-report-objects-criticism-and-defects-education/89644

level education in basic education. He has given the following suggestions about primary education:

1. All boys and girls of the age group of 6 to 14 years of age must be made as universal as the mandatory and free education system.
2. To make education compulsory, attendance officers should be appointed.
3. Basic education should be divided into two parts:
   (a) Junior Basic (6 to 11 years) and
   (b) Senior Basic (11 to 14 years). Etc.

4.3. Administration of Primary Education in India After Independence

After independence in the 20th century, the development of Indian education progressed through various challenging steps, which is being felt even in the early times of the 21st century. These challenges have increased even more when the population of India is continuously increasing. In such a situation, qualitative growth along with quantitative progress in elementary education becomes necessary. These challenges include the availability of resources, affordability to achieve it, the acceptability of teachers and administrators to provide equal opportunities to children of weaker and marginalised classes, and the adaptability of children and parents. Along with this, the accountability of teachers and educational administration is also being wished.

The child is the pivot of modern education around which the learning process revolves. The purpose of education, curriculum teaching method, teacher, and all educational systems of school is for the child's benefit. In modern education, various types of academic institutions are organised keeping in mind the child's development needs. An attempt to make primary education accessible to everyone has been made since independence but now the law of education for all could be implemented on April 1, 2010.

After the country's independence, special attention was given to education and emphasised on restructuring and renewal of Indian education. Several committees and commissions were set up to achieve this goal and their recommendations were implemented.

Article 45 of the Indian Constitution says, the state will endeavour to provide free and compulsory education to all children till they complete the age of fourteen, within ten years of the commencement of the constitution.[1]

1. Act, R. T. E. (2009). *The right of children to free and compulsory education act.* Published in Part II, Section, 1.

Here various efforts related to the upliftment of primary education after independence have been discussed.

4.3.1. Kothari Commission (1964-1966)

After independence, education was developed at a very rapid pace, but this development only became numeric and not qualitative. Along with this, the resolutions made to education in the constitution could not be fulfilled, as a result, dissatisfaction started in education. And in post-independence India, demand for the formation of a commission to investigate all aspects of education was started. Then on 14th July 1964, the Government of India announced the formation of the Education Commission under the chairmanship of Dr. Daulat Singh Kothari.[1] Kothari Commission has recommended the period of primary education for seven to eight years.

1. Inferior Stage (1 to 5 classes) and
2. Upper Primary Education (6 to 8 classes).

Kothari Commission has written in its report regarding the objectives of primary education that the purpose of modern elementary education is to enable the child to cope with the circumstances of future life, developing physical and mental training in such a way that it can become a useful citizen.

4.3.2. National Education Policy, 1968 and Primary Education

After discussions on the recommendations of the Kothari Education Commission (1964-66), the Government of India announced the National Education Policy (1968); accordingly, the guidelines for all levels of education and the working of the parties were determined.[2] The emphasis was placed at the primary level, according to which the scheme was planned to achieve the goal of Article 45 as soon as possible. It was also said that special programmes should be prepared for children leaving school.

4.3.3. National Education Policy (1986) and Revised Policy (1992)

Keeping in mind the goals shown in the Constitution, the National Education Policy of 1986 has given high priority to the universalisation of primary education so that all children up to 14 years can receive the minimum required education. For this, the segment split campaign started with the name of the blackboard campaign. It aims to upgrade the infrastructure of primary schools. The National Education Policy, 1986,

1. Kothari, D. S. (1970). *Education, science, and national development.* Asia Publishing House.
2. Kumar, A. (1991). *Current trends in Indian education.* APH Publishing.

was reviewed in 1992 and it was unveiled in its work plan and universal elementary education has the highest priority.[1] Emphasis on coordination in place of an emphasis on enrolment given the family and the child in mind, the work plan was prepared to ensure the teachers and the villagers that every child regularly attends a school or in a formal education system. Due to discouraging children and their parents such as the unexplained environment of the school, the unsatisfactory condition of the school building, and inadequate support for teaching aids were also given attention. Child-focused and work-based learning processes are adopted at the primary level. In the pre-service and service period, teacher education was restructured to upgrade primary education. Therefore, the National Education Policy 1986 and 1992 (revised) emphasised the three aspects of universal elementary education. That is:

1. Universal access and enrolment
2. The universal holding power of children up to the age of fourteen
3. To make qualitative improvements in education so that all the children can achieve a mandatory level of learning.

4.3.4. District Primary Education Programme

It was started in 1994. Under the District Primary Education Programme, special attention was given to the educationally backward districts in which female education is below the national average.[2] At the primary level (class 1-5 and all informal education), special attention was paid to this programme, with more emphasis on the education of girls and socially backward groups, etc.

4.3.5. Mid-day Meal Scheme (Nutritional Support for Primary Education)

This National Programme on Nutritional Support for Children in Primary Schools was implemented in 1995.[3] Mid-Day Meal is a scheme related to children whose purpose is to provide good food to the children and the objectives of this scheme are as follows:

1. Better development of children,

---

1. Aggarwal, J. C. (1992). *Education policy in India: 1992 and review 2000 and 2005.* Shipra Publications.
2. Varghese, N. V. (1996). *Decentralisation of educational planning in India: The case of the district primary education programme.* International Journal of Educational Development, 16(4), 355-365.
3. Joyita, 2013. The Mid-Day Meal Scheme. (2017, July 7). Retrieved from https://www.prsindia.org/theprsblog/mid-day-meal-scheme

2. More and more children can come to school,
3. Providing food to children in drought-affected areas, etc.

4.3.6 Sarva Shiksha Abhiyan (2001)

Presently the Sarva Shiksha Abhiyan programme is operated all over the country with the support of the Government of India.[1] Through this programme, the Government of India has decided to provide free education to all children of 6-14 years.[2] Before implementing Sarva Shiksha Abhiyan at the national level, its following objectives have been set:

1. Access to primary schools, education guarantee centres, alternate and back-to-school/camps for all children till 2003,
2. All children of 6-11-year-olds should complete elementary education up to Class 5 till 2007,
3. By 2010, all children up to 14 years should have completed eight years of education,
4. Providing satisfactory and quality elementary education for all children enrolled,
5. To eliminate all gender and social inequalities at the primary level till 2007, and to emphasise completing elementary education by 2010,
6. To ensure universal regular attendance of learners in schools by 2010.

Functions of Sarva Shiksha Abhiyan:

1. Establishing schools in such slums where there are no school facilities
2. Open extra classes
3. Construction of toilets in schools
4. To arrange drinking water
5. Maintenance allowance
6. Strengthen the infrastructure of schools
7. To remove teacher shortage

---

1. Sarva Siksha Abhiyan (SSA), *Manual for District- Level Functionaries. (2017).* MHRD, 1–199. Retrieved from https://darpg.gov.in/sites/default/files/Sarva%20 Siksha%20Abhiyan.pdf
2. Kainth, G. S. (2006). *A mission approach to Sarva Shiksha Abhiyan.* Economic and Political Weekly, 3288-3291.

8. Mobilisation of teaching-learning materials
9. Pay special attention to girls of weaker sections
10. Run many incentive schemes including free education, etc.

4.3.7. Early Childhood Care and Education (ECCE)

Before admission into school life, Early Childhood Care and Education (ECCE) centres have been set up to prepare the child's expected preparation.[1] Accepting the importance of ECCE in the National Education Policy, of 1986, special emphasis was laid on its establishment. It serves as an auxiliary service for primary education, the nutrition working women, and the deprived classes.

The joint responsibility of its operations in India is both government and non-governmental organisations. The development of children of 0-6 years is committed by the Ministry of Human Resource Development, Government of India. It operates ECCE centres by providing grants-in-aid to private entities.

Nationally organised national programme 'National Programme for the Education of Girls at Elementary Level' (NPEGEL) in places where school service is not available, community participation is said to open two ECCE centres per cluster.

1. Kaul, V. & Sankar, D. (2009). *Early childhood care and education in India.* Education for All Mid-Decade Assessment. New Delhi, India, National University of Educational Planning and Administration (NUEPA).

Right to Education and Quality of Primary Education in India

Chapter - V

Right to Education and Quality of Primary Education in India

5.1. Right to Education Act, 2009

5.1.1. Introduction

Education has been recognised as a fundamental human right all over the world, and those who are associated with education can develop skills, competence, and confidence to protect their rights. The right to education enables us to know what right we can claim. Thus, it can be considered as an initial effort to strengthen the social status of the individual.

The Right to Education Act, 2009 can also be considered an important effort in developing elementary education in India, which was accepted as a fundamental right for children between 6 and 14 years old. Many provisions in this act can prove to be milestones in the development of elementary education, which is the responsibility of the state to achieve. This Act talks about removing any economic hurdles necessary for the 8-year education of children of 6 to 14 years of age.[1]

In the Right to Education Act the detailed provisions are described in the following seven chapters:

Chapter 1: Preliminary

Chapter 2: Right to Free and Compulsory Education

Chapter 3: Duties of Appropriate Government, Local Authority and Parents

Chapter 4: Responsibilities of Schools and Teachers

---

1. Jha, P., & Parvati, P. (2010). *Right to Education Act 2009: critical gaps and challenges.* Economic and Political Weekly, 20-23.

Chapter 5: Curriculum and Completion of Elementary Education

Chapter 6: Protection of Rights of Children

Chapter 7: Miscellaneous[1]

Different 'articles' and 'sections' related to education are described in each of its chapters. This policy document is a list of activities to achieve the fundamental rights of children, as well as sets minimum standards to ensure the educational rights of children for the state and schools. It has been described as a policy document to clearly state the needs of India's education system, which means that every child aged 6 to 14 years is entitled to free and compulsory primary education.

This Act insists on removing any financial barrier for any child to receive eight years of elementary education in a neighborhood school. It describes the basic facilities of schools as well as their minimum standards and standards. Through this Act, attention has also been focused on increasing community participation in schools, for which the establishment of school management committees, in which parents, teachers, and elected representatives are mentioned.

In the present study, various features of the Right to Education Act and their objectives are discussed. It is using the 4A framework developed by former UN rapporteur, Katrina Tomasevski, in making education a meaningful right.[2]

5.1.2. Some important provisions of the Right to Education Act

A. Availability

1. About the right of the child to free and compulsory education:

   Section 3(1) of the RTE Act provides the right to free and compulsory education to every child between the ages of 6 to 14 years. Under this act, it is stated that children can take education till the completion of elementary education in a neighbourhood school.

   Section 3(2) states that no child shall be liable to pay fees or charges, which may prevent him from pursuing elementary education.[3]

---

1. Sarangapani, P. M., Mehendale, A., Mukhopadhyay, R., & Namala, A. (2014). *Inclusion of marginalised children in private unaided schools.* The RTE Act, 2009.
2. Helfer, L. R., & Austin, G. W. (2011). *Human rights and intellectual property: Mapping the global interface.* Cambridge University Press.
3. Act, R. T. E. (2009). *The Right of Children to Free and Compulsory Education Act 2009.* The Gazette of India.

2. About standards for recognition of schools:

   The RTE Act mentions the following points for determining the norms and standards of schools:

   (a) Minimum number of working hours per week for teachers
   (b) Minimum number of working days
   (c) Instructional hours in an academic year
   (d) Guidelines relating to school building
   (e) The ideal pupil-teacher ratio
   (f) Library facility
   (g) Guidelines on teaching or play material

   As per Section 18 (1) of the RTE Act, no school will be able to operate the school without obtaining a certificate of recognition from the competent local authority.[1]

3. About the establishment of additional schools:

   Section 6 of the RTE Act says, that within three years from the commencement of this Act, the appropriate government and local authority shall establish within the limits of such area or neighbourhood as may be prescribed.[2]

   As per Section 7(1) of the RTE Act, both the Central and State Governments shall have concurrent financial responsibilities to implement the provisions of this Act.

   According to Section 7(2) of the RTE Act, the estimate of capital and recurring expenditure required for the implementation of this Act shall be prepared by the Central Government.[3]

4. About appointment of qualified teachers:

   According to Section 23(1) of the RTE Act, any person with the minimum qualification prescribed by the educational authority

1. Right to Education (2014). Section 18. No school to be established without obtaining a certificate of recognition. Retrieved from http://righttoeducation.in/forums/suggest-rte-amendments/section-18-no-school-to-be-established-without-obtaining-certificate-of-recognition
2. Right to Education (2014). Section 6. Duty of appropriate Government and local authority to establish a school. Retrieved from http://righttoeducation.in/forums/suggest-rte-amendments/ section-6-duty-of-appropriate-government-and-local-authority-to-establish-school#forum-topic-top
3. The Right of Children to Free and Compulsory Education Act, 2009. Clarification on Provisions. Retrieved from https://mhrd.gov.in/sites/upload_files/mhrd/files/upload_document/RTE_Section_wise_rationale_rev_0.pdf

authorised by the Central Government will be eligible for appointment as a teacher.[1]

B. Affordability

1. About disallowing capitation fees and screening procedures:

   Section 13(1) of the RTE Act expressly prohibits any school or individual from collecting any capitation fee from children and carrying out any screening process of a child or its parent or guardian.[2]

2. About special training-related provisions:

   According to Section 4 of this Act, children who are more than 6 years old and have never been able to enter any school or have completed primary education will be given admission to the class according to their age.[3]

3. About provision relating to admission of children from weaker and disadvantaged groups:

   According to Section 12(1) (c) of the Act, private unaided schools will have to admit 25% of the class's total children to weaker and disadvantaged groups.[4]

4. About provision regarding the representation of the School Management Committee:

   According to Section 21(1) of the RTE Act, schools have to constitute a school management committee in which elected representatives of local government, parents or guardians of children, and teachers are represented. At the same time, it further states that three-fourths of the committee members will be guardians, which will also include proportionate representation

---

1. Right to Education, (2014). Section 23. Qualifications for appointment and terms and conditions of service of teachers. Retrieved from http://righttoeducation.in/forums/suggest-rte-amendments/section-23-qualifications-for-appointment-and-terms-and-conditions-of-service-of-teachers
2. Right to Education, (2014). Section 13. No capitation fee and screening procedure for admission. Retrieved from http://righttoeducation.in/forums/suggest-rte-amendments/section-13-no-capitation-fee-and-screening-procedure-for-admission
3. Right to Education, (2014). Section 4. Special provisions for children not admitted to, or who have not completed elementary education. Retrieved from http://righttoeducation.in/forums/ suggest-rte-amendments/section-4-special-provisions-for-children-not-admitted-to-or-who-have-not-completed-elementary-education
4. Right to Education, (2014). Section 12. Extent of school's responsibility for free and compulsory education. Retrieved from http://righttoeducation.in/forums/suggest-rte-amendments/section-12-extent-of-schools-responsibility-for-free-and-compulsory-education

of the parents of children belonging to weaker and disadvantaged groups. Further, as per this provision of the RTE Act, 50% of the women in the school management committees will be women. This section of the RTE Act will not be applicable in unaided schools, which are not receiving any kind of aid or grant by the local government or authority.[1]

C. Acceptability

1. About provision for the development of national curriculum:

   According to Section 7(6A) of the RTE Act, the central government should develop a national curriculum framework with the help of the educational officials appointed by the state governments.[2]

2. About provision regarding holding back or expulsion of children from school and prohibition of physical and mental harassment:

   Under Section 16 of the RTE Act, no child will be held back in any class of the school or shall not be expelled until the completion of his primary education.[3]

   Section 17(1) of the RTE Act states that no child shall be subjected to corporal punishment or mental harassment.[4]

3. About the duties of teachers:

   The duties of teachers are described under Section 24 of the RTE Act, in which regularity, punctuality, completion of syllabus within a specified time, assessing the learning ability of each child and providing appropriate instruction, etc. is included.[5]

D. Adaptability

1. About students belonging to disadvantaged groups: Various

---

1. Right to Education, (2014). Section 21. School Management Committee. Retrieved from http:// righttoeducation.in/forums/suggest-rte-amendments/section-21-school-management- committee
2. Right to Education, (2014). Section 7. Sharing of financial and other responsibilities. Retrieved from http·//righttoeducation.in/forums/suggest-rteamendments/section-7-sharing-of-financial-and-other-responsibilities
3. The Gazette of India, (2019). The Right of Children to Free and Compulsory Education (Amendment) Act, 2019. Retrieved from https://mhrd.gov.in/sites/upload_files/mhrd/files/ upload_ document/rte_2019.pdf
4. The Right of Children to Free and Compulsory Education Act, (2009). Clarification on Provisions. Retrieved from https://mhrd.gov.in/sites/upload_files/mhrd/files/upload_document/RTE_Section_ wise_rationale_rev_0.pdf
5. Right to Education, (2014). Section 24. Duties of teachers and redressal of grievances. Retrieved from http://righttoeducation.in/forums/suggest-rte-amendments/section-24-duties-of-teachers-and-redressal-of-grievances

provisions have been described under the RTE Act regarding the admission and security of students belonging to socially disadvantaged groups.

2. About the right to transfer to another school:

   Section 5(1) of the RTE Act gives the right to transfer any child who is getting primary education in a government or government-aided school, to another school.[1]

5.2. Qualitative Primary Education

For any country's national development, improving the quality of education there is very important. Hence, there is a strong thrust for quality improvement and education upgrading in developing countries. Efforts to improve the quality of education include improvement of the internal efficiency of the system, making it more relevant to the current needs of the people, updating the curriculum and syllabus, and the production of quality textbooks and instructional materials. Science education and structural reorganisation of the educational system have received special attention for qualitative improvement.[2]

Quality of learning is a major issue in elementary education, according to a report; children are unable to adopt the level of classroom-appropriate learning. According to Pratham's Annual Status of Education Report 2013, about 78% of the students of Class 3 and about 50% of the students of Class 5 cannot read Class 2 books. If we talk about the subject, arithmetic is also a cause for concern, because only 26% children of in Class 5 can solve division questions.[3] According to ASER 2017, only 37.4% of youth aged 14-18 years old could do division and 49.6% of youth could read English sentences in Varanasi.[4] Without immediate help, these children will not progress effectively in the education system; therefore, improving the quality of learning in schools is a major challenge for the present and future for the Central and State Governments.

Mehrotra (2005) says that the private sector, public provision, and funding requirements are more in India. Along with this, to take qualitative

1. The Gazette of India, (2009). The Right of Children to Free and Compulsory Education Act, (2009). Retrieved from https://mhrd.gov.in/sites/upload_files/mhrd/files/upload_document/rte.pdf
2. Bhagia, N., Briggs, D., & Bhagia, S. (1990). *Educational administration in India and other developing countries: Challenges, tasks and training.* Commonwealth Publishers.
3. India, A. S. E. R. (2014). *Annual status of education report (rural) 2013.* ASER Centre, New Delhi.
4. India, A. S. E. R. (2017). *Annual status of education report (rural) 2013.* ASER Centre, New Delhi.

improvement in both public and private sectors keeping in view the uneven nature of the private sector which includes aided private schools, unaided private schools, and unaccredited private schools, etc. If the private sector progresses at the elementary level, then its income will also increase, whether the government subsidises it or not. In addition, better regulation is also needed for the private sectors at all levels, i.e., primary, secondary, and tertiary.[1]

Puar (2012) has emphasised various aspects of the Right to Education Act and has suggested some ways to improve them, e.g., children above 14 years of age should also be covered under this Act, the Common school system should be converted into a Model school system, and efforts should be made to increase the role of parents or guardians, and so on.[2]

In the Journal **(Yojana, August 2012),** Chavan says in 'Elementary education: access to what?' about standardisation of data that, Indian sampling and data were not up to OECD (Organisation for Economic Co-operation and Development) standards. PISA (Programme for International Student Assessment) 2009+ tests, remember that only school-going children aged 15 participated in the test. Among 75 participants, only one Kirghizstan is in 75th place, ranked below India. A footnote in the report says that Indian sampling and data were not up to OECD standards. We ran a race, got second last, and then failed the dope test.[3]

The theme of this article by Satyarthi **(Yojana, Nov.2012)** is 'Education for Empowerment'. According to Satyarthi, Child Labour is the biggest impediment to school enrolment, retention, and attainment of quality education. In the present era of globalisation that thrives on information and technology, the notion of education has undergone a complete change over the last 25 years. Earlier the rhetoric was "Education for Employment". Today it stands revised to "Education for Empowerment".[4]

In the Journal **(Yojana, August 2012)**, Yash Pal says in 'An Optimistic Future for Indian Education' about 'Quality Education in India' that, children are forced to score high in mindless races of competition as they operate through the examination system. Apart from all this, the large industry of coaching classes plays a very important role in killing the curiosity and creativity of the children.[5]

1. Mehrotra, S. K. (Ed.). (2005). *Universalizing elementary education in India: Uncaging the 'tiger' economy.* Oxford University Press, USA.
2. Puar, S. S. (2012). *Right to Education Act: A critical analysis.* International Journal of Educational and Psychological Research (IJEPR), 1(2), 27-30.
3. Chavan, M. (August 2012). *Elementary education: Access to what?* Yojana, 56, 53-55.
4. Satyarthi, K. (November 2012). *Preparing for the new child labour law.* Yojana, 56, 19-21.
5. Pal, Y. (August 2012). *An optimistic future for Indian Education.* Yojana, 56, 5-7.

Pritchett et al., (2006) talk about the voucher system in their book and say, under the voucher proposal, parents would be given 'vouchers' by the government, which they would be free to take to the school of their choice - including private schools - as payment for educating their children.[1]

Govinda and Bandyopadhyay (2008) in their book talk about community involvement and say, that the last few years have seen the emergence of a variety of mechanisms to facilitate community involvement in school governance such as School Development Management Committees, empowered School Management Committees, Committees of Panchayati Raj Institutions through the new Jana Shiksha Adhiniyam, and the revamped Village Education Committees in several states. But without administrative reform in every department related to education, all these efforts are likely to be ineffective. According to the same UNICEF report (2004), over 20% of India's working children are from Uttar Pradesh, most of whom work at odd jobs, such as in factories and the carpet industry, for meager wages.[2]

Bandyopadhyay and Behera (2010) say that various researches show that pre-primary education is very important for the development of young children, and helps in admission to primary or formal education (Kaul 2002). It can be understood in this way that qualitative pre-primary education is also necessary to promote inclusive education and increase enrollment. The Ministry of Women and Child Development is responsible for the development of pre-primary education in India, while the Ministry of Human Resource Development is responsible for the development of primary education. We also have to understand that the education of 3-6-year-olds has not been accepted as a fundamental right in India, i.e., pre-primary education has not been made legally mandatory. Therefore, keeping in mind the important role of pre-primary education in the lives of children, it needs to be accepted immediately based on development parameters.[3]

Bandyopadhyay and Dev (2011) in their work say that the school management committees need to focus on tasks related to tracking children's progress and monitoring important indicators. The school development plans must be shared in Gram Sabha (village council meetings) organised from time to time. SMCs should contribute to a system of social audits at the local level.[4]

1. *Ibid.*
2. Govinda, R., & Bandyopadhyay, M. (2008). *Access to elementary education in India.* Consortium for Research on Educational Access, Transitions and Equity (CREATE).
3. Brief, C. I. P. (2010). Pre-Primary Education in India.
4. Brief, C. I. P. (2011). Effective School Management Committees.

Bandyopadhyay et al., (2011) in their work say that it is necessary to maintain the student-teacher ratio, of 30:1 to 35:1 in all schools and no school should hide its information so that this deficiency can be overcome. Current programmes related to teacher education and qualitative improvements are inadequate and need to be focused on.[1]

In **The Hindu (2013)**, the author says, that the wave of privatisation of education is a dangerous trend for universalisation of education and the constitutional right of children coming from marginalised sections.

5.3. Status of Primary Education in India

The Hindu, 2014 (India's National Newspaper) says, as per the ninth Annual Status of Education Report (ASER) 2014, 29 percent of enrolments in the 6 to 14 age group are in private schools in rural areas. This is an increase of 10% in seven years from 18.7% to 29% during the years 2006 to 2013.[2]

According to the **Brookings Institute Report, 2015**, in India, about 29% of primary-level children leave school without completing 5 years of education, while the number of children leaving school at the upper primary level is about 43%.

Urvashi Sahni (2015) in her work, "Primary Education in India: Progress and Challenges" says that, at the national level, 29% of children drop out of school before completing five years of primary school and this figure rises to 43% at upper primary level. Only 42% of children complete high school. India is one of the five countries in the world with the highest number of children outside primary school with about 1.4 million 6 to 11-year-olds never attending school. In many ways, resources related to primary schools do not meet the needs of the entire population. There is a shortage of about 6,89,000 teachers in primary schools, 74% of schools do not have drinking water and 53% of schools do not have functional toilets for girls.

According to ASER 2018, in every 10 government primary schools in India, 4 schools were found to have less than 60 children enrolled during the visit. The number of such schools increased steadily from the year 2009 to the year 2018. The number of such schools increased to 26.1% in 2009, 30% in 2011, 33.1% in 2013, 39.8% in 2016 and 43.3% in 2018.[3]

---

1. Brief, C. I. P. (2011). Teachers and Teaching in India.
2. The Hindu, (2014, November 26). Retrieved from http://en.kiosko.net/in/2014-11-26/np/hindu. html.Pg.11
3. Center, A. S. E. R. (2018). *Annual Status of Education Report.* New Delhi: ASER Center.

Some important points of the survey conducted by the Annual Status of Education Report (ASER), 2018 are shown below, based on which we can understand the current state of elementary education in India.

Table 5.1: Status of Primary Education in India

Year	Percentage of children in class 3 who can read class 2 level book		Percentage of children in class 5 who can read class 2 level book	
	Government	Private	Government	Private
2012	16.7	33.8	41.7	61.2
2014	17.2	37.8	42.2	62.6
2016	19.3	38.0	41.7	63.0
2018	20.9	40.6	44.2	65.1

Source: ASER, 2018.

Table 5.2: Status of Primary Education in India

Year	Percentage of children in class 3 who can do subtraction		Percentage of children in class 5 who can do division	
	Government	Private	Government	Private
2012	19.8	43.4	20.3	37.8
2014	17.2	43.4	20.7	39.3
2016	20.3	44.1	21.1	38.0
2018	20.9	43.5	22.7	39.8

Source: ASER, 2018.

Table 5.3: Availability of various resources at primary schools in India till the year 2018

Resources	Percentage
Drinking Water	74.8
Usable toilet	74.2
Usable toilets for girls	66.4
Connection of electricity	75.0

Source: ASER, 2018.

5.4. Status of Primary Education in Uttar Pradesh

Uttar Pradesh is an important state of historical and cultural heritage, political awareness, population freedom movement, etc. The population of Uttar Pradesh is highest in all the states of India and most of the people here live in villages. About 16.17% of the total population of India lives in the state of Uttar Pradesh and this number is about 20.42 crores. Geographically, the state of Uttar Pradesh ranks fourth after Rajasthan,

Madhya Pradesh, and Maharashtra and covers about 7.34% of India's land area. Uttar Pradesh is spread over an area of 240.982 sq. km. Uttar Pradesh is a developing state but it has lagged behind some states in the field of education.[1]

Problems arising out of the absence of elementary education do not end here. The next step is - Child Labour. According to UNICEF, in 2011, about 28 million children of 5 to 14 years in India are working.[2] According to various institutions, any child who does not attend school is child labour.

The Education Development Index in the education sector is released every year by the National University of Educational Planning and Administration. The standards of measurement of the Education Development Index include accessibility of education, basic infrastructure, quality of teachers, and outcomes. Through this, we can easily understand the progress of elementary education in India.

According to this report, the state of Uttar Pradesh is constantly deteriorating from the perspective of elementary education in comparison to all the states and union territories of India. From the perspective of the Composite Educational Development Index, the state of Uttar Pradesh has been ranked 23rd in the year 2009-10, 29th in 2010-11, 32nd in 2011-12, 34th in 2012-13, and 35th in 2013-14, which is the lowest in all states and union territory of India.[3]

As per the 2015-16 report of the District Information System for Education (DISE), there was a steady increase in the number of school dropouts of upper primary level children in India every year during the year 2012-15, with percentage rates of 3.13, 3.77 and 4.03 while in high schools it was 14.54, 17.86 and 17.06.[4] At the same time, it is also necessary to note that enrolment of boys and girls in primary schools steadily decreased during the year 2012-15.[5]

As of 2014, the literacy rate of children aged 7 years or over in India was 75.4%. From the perspective of the teacher-student ratio in the year 2015-16 in Uttar Pradesh, there was one teacher per 39 students in the

1. Social Demography, (2011). Retrieved from http://up.gov.in/Social-Demography.pdf
2. UNICEF, I., and UNICEF, (2011). *The situation of children in India: a profile.* New Delhi: UNICEF.
3. Report of Workshop on Educational Development Index (EDI) (2014, July 30). NUEPA, 2014. Retrieved from http://www.dise.in/Downloads/EDI%20workshop%20report.pdf
4. School Education in India, (2016). NUEPA, 2016. Retrieved from http://www.dise.in/Downloads/Publications/Documents/U-DISE-SchoolEducationInIndia-2015-16.pdf
5. *Ibid.*

primary level class, and one teacher was available per 31 students in the upper primary level class.[1] This situation is the lowest level in all the states and centrally administered regions of India along with not fulfilling the provisions of the Right to Education Act.

From the point of view of the attendance of children in schools, during the year 2014, the attendance of children in primary schools in Uttar Pradesh was 77% which is more than just Arunachal Pradesh (70%) and Goa (71%) in all states and union territories of India, and the attendance of children in upper primary level schools of Uttar Pradesh was just 48%, which is more than just Daman & Diu (38%) in all the states and union territories of India.[2]

The Right to Education Act was enacted in April 2010 to provide free and compulsory education to all children of 6-14 years in India. For the development of elementary education, it is very important to keep in mind that the development of education should be quantitative as well as qualitative. To understand whether the development of elementary education in the state of Uttar Pradesh from the year 2010 to 2014 has been quantitative as well as qualitative or not, we should look at the data in the 'Annual Status of Education Report (ASER)'.

Table 5.4: Status of Primary Education in Uttar Pradesh % Children in Std. II and III at different Reading levels by school type 2010-2014

Year	% Children in Std. II who can read at least letters			% Children in Std. III who can read at least words		
	Govern-ment	Private	Government & Private	Govern-ment	Private	Government & Private
2010	77.2	91.1	82.4	56.1	77.8	64.2
2011	66.1	89.7	77.4	40.1	74.4	55.6
2012	55.6	87.9	72.2	27.1	69.3	47.8
2013	53.5	87.4	70.1	31.6	73.9	52.3
2014	50.0	86.4	69.1	27.9	71.7	50.8

Source: ASER, 2014.

Table 5.4 shows that during the year 2010-14 in government schools, the number of children in Std. II who can read letters has decreased from 77.2% in the year 2010 to 50% in the year 2014. At the same time, the

1. Source, D. Government of India (website: http://mhrd.gov.in/statist). *Educational Statistics at a Glance (2018).* Published By: Government of India, Ministry of Human Resource Development, New Delhi.
2. Elementary Education in India, (2016). NUEPA, 2016. Retrieved from http://dise.in/Downloads/ Elementary-STRC-2015-16/Elementary-State_Report_Cards_2015-16.pdf

number of children in Std. 3 who can read words has come down from 56.1% in the year 2010 to 27.9% in the year 2014.[1]

Table 5.5: Status of Primary Education in Uttar Pradesh

Year	% Children in Std. IV who can read at least Std. I level text			% Children in Std. V who can read Std. II level text		
	Government	Private	Government & Private	Government	Private	Government & Private
2010	46.2	69.5	55.0	36.0	58.4	44.1
2011	32.5	67.6	48.9	29.9	60.3	43.3
2012	25.4	67.9	46.9	25.6	59.6	42.7
2013	29.4	70.7	49.8	25.5	63.8	43.6
2014	26.9	67.6	48.1	26.8	61.4	44.6

Source: ASER, 2014.

Table 5.5 shows that during the year 2010-14 in government schools, the number of children in Std. IV who can read at least Std. I-level text has decreased from 46.2% in the year 2010 to 26.9% in the year 2014. At the same time, the number of children in Std. V who can read Std. II level text has come down from 36% in the year 2010 to 26.8% in the year 2014.

Table 5.6: Status of Primary Education in Uttar Pradesh % Children in Std. II and III at different Arithmetic levels by school type 2010-2014

Year	% Children in Std. II who can recognize numbers 1-9 and more			% Children in Std. III who can recognize numbers 10-99 and more		
	Government	Private	Government & Private	Government	Private	Government & Private
2010	76.8	91.2	82.2	51.0	73.9	59.6
2011	69.5	91.1	79.9	36.9	69.3	51.6
2012	62.9	92.2	77.9	25.1	67.2	45.7
2013	63.4	91.1	77.0	30.6	72.9	51.2
2014	59.3	89.6	75.3	28.8	72.6	51.7

Source: ASER, 2014.

Table 5.6 shows that during the year 2010-14 in government schools, the number of children in Std. II who can recognise numbers 1-9 and more has decreased from 76.8% in the year 2010 to 59.3% in the year 2014. At the same time, the number of children in Std. III who can recognise numbers 10-99 and more has come down from 51.0% in the year 2010 to 28.8% in the year 2014.

1. ASER. (2014). Uttar Pradesh. *Analysis Based on Data From Households.* 69 Out of 69 Districts.

Table 5.7: Status of Primary Education in Uttar Pradesh % Children in Std. IV and V at different Arithmetic levels by school type 2010-2014

Year	% Children in Std. IV who can do at least subtraction			% Children in Std. V who can do division		
	Government	Private	Government & Private	Government	Private	Government & Private
2010	36.6	55.0	41.1	18.7	36.3	25.0
2011	21.6	50.3	35.1	12.1	33.4	21.5
2012	12.1	48.7	30.6	9.1	33.3	21.3
2013	20.3	56.0	38.0	11.2	42.3	26.3
2014	17.8	52.7	35.9	12.1	38.7	25.8

Source: ASER, 2014.

Table 5.7 shows that during the year 2010-14 in government schools, the number of children in Std. IV who can do at least subtraction has decreased from 36.6% in the year 2010 to 17.8% in the year 2014. At the same time, the number of children in Std. V who can divide has come down from 18.7% in the year 2010 to 12.1% in the year 2014.

According to ASER, 2018, in Uttar Pradesh, attendance of children in primary schools was less than 60% based on random day visits. According to ASER, 2018, in Uttar Pradesh, more than 60% of children in Class 3 cannot read words yet.

Table 5.8: Percentage of children enrolled in different types of schools in Uttar Pradesh by age group and gender in 2018

Age Group	Government	Private	Other	Not in School	Total
Age 6-14: All	44.3	49.7	1.3	4.9	100
Age 11-14: All	38.5	54.3	1.1	6.2	100
Age 11-14: Boys	35.8	58.2	1.0	5.0	100
Age 11-14: Girls	41.5	49.9	1.2	7.4	100

Source: ASER, 2018.

Table 5.9: Status of primary education in Uttar Pradesh

Year	Percentage of children in class 3 who can read class 2 level text			Percentage of children in class 3 who can do at least subtraction		
	Government	Private	Government & Private	Government	Private	Government & Private
2012	6.5	31.5	18.8	6.7	32.0	19.1
2014	6.0	36.0	21.7	6.6	38.5	23.3
2016	7.2	36.6	22.6	7.9	37.5	23.4
2018	12.3	45.4	28.3	11.2	43.7	26.9

Source: ASER, 2014.

Table 5.10: Status of primary education in Uttar Pradesh

Year	Percentage of children in class 5 who can read class 2 level text			Percentage of children in class 8 who can read class 2 level text		
	Government	Private	Government & Private	Government	Private	Government & Private
2012	25.6	59.6	42.7	57.3	81.8	69.7
2014	26.8	61.4	44.6	59.3	81.9	70.9
2014	24.3	61.2	43.1	56.3	78.6	67.9
2018	36.2	68.8	52.4	62.0	85.0	73.8

Source: ASER, 2018.

Table 5.11: Status of primary education in Uttar Pradesh

Year	Percentage of children in class 5 who can do division			Percentage of children in class 8 who can do division		
	Government	Private	Government & Private	Government	Private	Government & Private
2012	9.1	33.3	21.3	24.4	48.4	36.6
2014	12.1	38.7	25.8	30.5	56.6	43.9
2014	10.4	34.6	22.7	25.5	48.4	37.4
2018	17.0	42.9	29.8	32.0	56.5	44.6

Source: ASER, 2018.

A survey conducted by NITI Aayog in India regarding Elementary Education through the School Education Quality Index (SEQI)

Among larger states, this index has given Kerala the highest 76.6% for the overall performance score for the year 2016-17, while Uttar Pradesh has the lowest 36.4%.

Under the category of learning, access to resources and facilities, etc., a huge difference was seen in various states and union territories in this index of outcomes. Karnataka got the highest 81.9% score in the big states under the outcomes category, while Uttar Pradesh got the least 34.1%.

In the year 2016-17, various states and union territories submitted their report to NITI Aayog from the perspective of children going from primary education to upper primary education. According to NITI Aayog's SEQI report, the transition rate of children from primary to upper primary schools in 27 states was above 90% while Uttar Pradesh, Jharkhand, and Bihar had the lowest transition rates of 77.9, 76.3 and 76.1% respectively.

According to the SEQI report, 26 states and union territories have referenced the unique IDs of the teachers of the state under the electronic database, whereas no such information of the teachers of the two states namely Uttar Pradesh and Jharkhand are referenced in the electronic database.[1]

Among all the states and union territories of India, Uttar Pradesh (49.7%) is the only state after Haryana (55.3%) where enrollment of 6-14 year-old children in private primary schools was highest in the year 2018.[2]

5.5. Status of Primary Education in Varanasi

Located in the eastern part of Uttar Pradesh, Varanasi district is financially a wealthy district. Here the population density is high.

Varanasi district is one of the seven districts in the state of Uttar Pradesh where the maximum enrolments of 6-14-year-old children are in private schools in the year 2013. About 62.3% of children in the Varanasi district are enrolled in private schools.[3]

During the year 2013-14, the enrolment rate of 6-14-year-old children in private schools in the Varanasi district decreased to 56.2% from the previous year.[4]

The number of school dropouts of 6-14-year-olds in Varanasi district in the year 2013 is the lowest in the entire state of Uttar Pradesh. In the year 2013, the number of school dropouts in Varanasi district is about 0.4%.

The number of school dropouts of 6-14-year-olds in the Varanasi district increased to 3.1% during the year 2013-14 over the previous year, which has emerged as a very worrying aspect for the proper implementation of the right to education.

Table 5.12: Status of primary education at Varanasi in 2018

Percentage of children enrolled in private schools	55.2
Percentage of children not enrolled in any school	2.5
Percentage of children in classes 3 to 5 who can read class 2 level text	50.8
Percentage of children in classes 3 to 5 who can do at least subtraction	50.0
Percentage of children in classes 6 to 8 who can read class 2 level text	74.9
Percentage of children in classes 6 to 8 who can do division	41.8

Source: ASER, 2018.

1. Aayog, N. I. T. I. (2019). School Education Quality Index.
2. Center, A. S. E. R. (2018). *Annual Status of Education Report.* New Delhi: ASER Center.
3. ASER. (2013). *District Performance Tables: Uttar Pradesh.*
4. ASER. (2014). *District Performance Tables: Uttar Pradesh.*

Status of Right to Education in Varanasi

Chapter - VI

Status of Right to Education in Varanasi

The data collected can be meaningless until it is properly presented and systematically analyzed to convert it into knowledge. Through data analysis, the researcher wants to know what he or she has discovered in the empirical research project. He or she analyses and interprets the data collected to determine its meaning and implications (Sedisa, 2008). The purpose of this chapter is to systematically present and analyze data collected on the extent to which indicators of administration can be used to improve the quality of the provision of primary education in the Varanasi Municipal Corporation (VMC) area. It also aimed at finding problems with current RTE implementation along with respondent suggestions on how to improve the educational administration of the city under study. The data has been analyzed specifically to address the research questions presented in chapter one of the book. The data is presented in the form of tables and figures, which are also referenced and interpreted for easy understanding. This empirical study schedule is based on data collected from 351 respondents, where 117 parents of students along with 234 teachers and administrators belonging to primary schools under Varanasi Municipal Corporation through interview schedule, analysis of which is presented below.

6.1. Demographic and Socio-Economic Profile of the Parents of Children

In this section, the demographic and socio-economic profiles of the parents of primary school children in Varanasi have been dealt with briefly with the help of a table. And for easy comprehension necessary figures have also been generated.

Table 6.1 shows the introductory demographic and socio-economic profile of the Parents of the primary school children surveyed using a scheduled questionnaire. A total of 117 parents were interviewed during the primary survey, which included 73(62.39%) men and 44(37.60%) women. The task of selecting 117 parents was done through the 'Taro Yamane' formula, i.e. n = N/ {1+N (e^2)}. The total number of private, privately aided, and government schools under the Varanasi Municipal Corporation is 166 (NIEPA, n.d.). In Table 6.1, we can see that most of the parents have an income of Rs 1 lakh to 2 lakh (38.5%) annually followed by parents with Rs.50 thousand to 1 lakh (27.4%), which can be easily understood through the Figure 6.1. These parents are classified under a total of five occupations, which can be seen as government service, private service, business, agriculture, and other work. It has the highest number of self-employed people (29.9%) which is followed by the number of parents associated with other work (19.7%) and agriculture (17.9%), shown in Figure 6.2. The areas covered during the primary survey were urban (62.4%) and semi-urban (37.6%). Schools can be seen as government (35%), private aided (10.3%) and private unaided (54.7%).

Table 6.1: Introductory Characteristics of Parents of Children

Demographic Profile	Parameters	Number of Participants	Percentage of Participants
Gender	*Male*	73	62.39
	Female	44	37.60
	Total	**117**	**100**
Annual Income	*Up to 50000 Rupees*	24	20.5
	50000-100000 Rupees	32	27.4
	100000-200000 Rupees	45	38.5
	200000-500000 Rupees	15	12.8
	500000 and above	1	0.9
	Total	**117**	**100**
Occupation	*Government Service*	16	13.7
	Private Service	22	18.8
	Business	35	29.9
	Agriculture	21	17.9
	Others	23	19.7
	Total	**117**	**100**
Location	*Urban*	73	62.4
	Semi-urban	44	37.6
	Total	**117**	**100**
Type of School	*Government*	41	35.0
	Private-aided	12	10.3
	Private-unaided	64	54.7
	Total	**117**	**100**

Source:- Field Survey, 2017-18.

Figure 6.1: Parent's Annual Income.

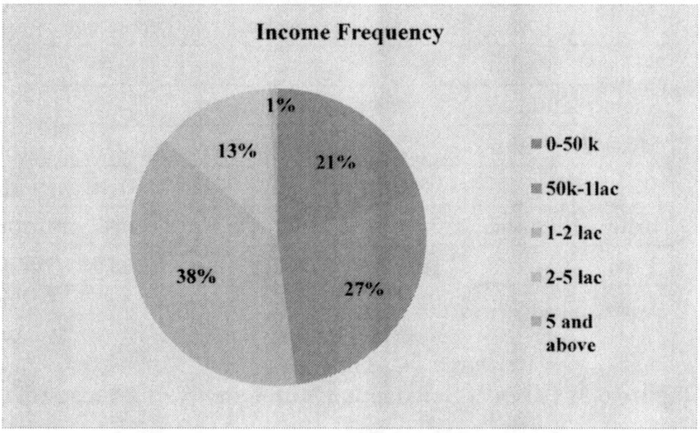

Figure 6.2: Parent's Occupation.

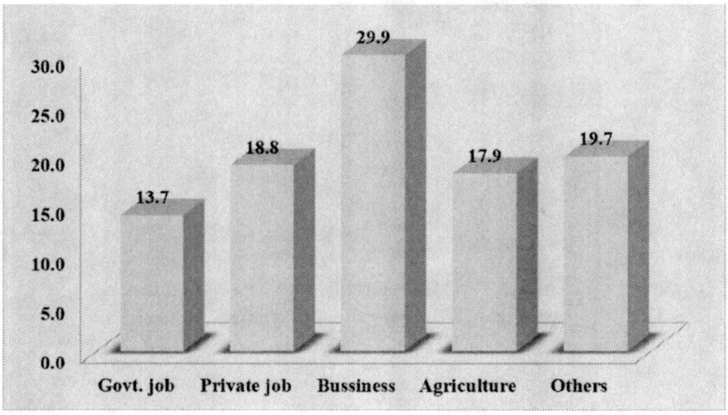

6.2. Parent's Views and Attitudes towards various indicators of 4As and Accountability

In this section of data analysis, an attempt has been made to analyze the attitude of parents towards the 4A scheme and awareness about the accountability of different aspects of the RTE Act in the city of Varanasi through numerous tables and appropriate figures and graphs.

A. Availability

As evident from Table 6.2, the majority of the parents (35%) are moderately satisfied about the primary education of their children followed by parents (34.2%) who think that they are slightly satisfied about the primary education system of the Varanasi. Only 6% of parents are satisfied with the quality of their child's education, which is also can be understood easily with the help of Figure 6.3.

Table 6.2: Quality of Education

	Frequency	Percentage
Not at all satisfied	16	13.7
Slightly satisfied	40	34.2
Moderately satisfied	41	35.0
Very satisfied	13	11.1
Extremely satisfied	7	6.0
Total	**117**	**100.0**

Source:- Field Survey, 2017-18.

Figure 6.3: Parent's Satisfaction with Quality of Education.

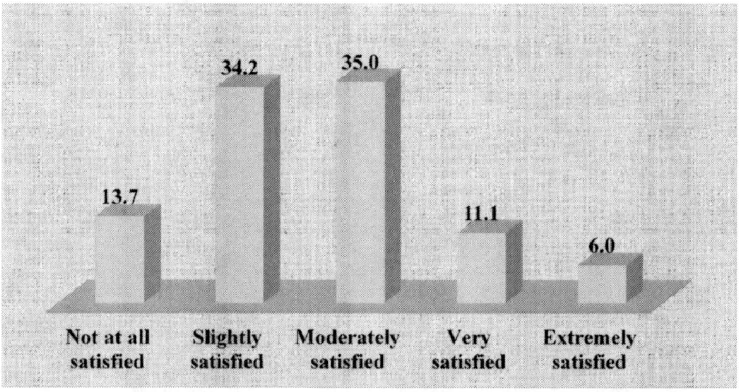

Table 6.3: Opportunities to Participate in Physical Education

	Frequency	Percentage
Not at all influential	7	6.0
Slightly influential	36	30.8
Somewhat influential	46	39.3
Very influential	19	16.2
Extremely influential	9	7.7
Total	**117**	**100.0**

Source:- Field Survey, 2017-18.

In Table 6.3, we can see most of the parents think that the opportunities to participate in the physical education of their children's school are somewhat influential (39.3%) followed by slightly influential (30.8%).

Table 6.4: School Facilities (cleanliness and maintenance)

	Frequency	Percentage
Very undesirable	1	0.9
Undesirable	25	21.4
Neutral	41	35.0
Desirable	38	32.5
Very desirable	12	10.3
Total	**117**	**100.0**

Source:- Field Survey, 2017-18.

Along with the resources available in schools, its cleanliness and maintenance are also an important issue. In this regard, it was seen at various times that, many children leave schools just because the toilets, tables, chairs, etc., are not kept clean. In this regard, efforts were made to know the views of the parents. It can be seen in Table 6.4 that most of the parents are neither very concerned nor very happy in this regard (35%). After this, 32.5% of the parents considered the schools to be good in this regard.

B. Affordability

Table 6.5: Children's Safety in School

	Frequency	Percentage
Strongly disagree	3	2.6
Disagree	16	13.7
Neither agree or disagree	56	47.9
Agree	41	35.0
Strongly agree	1	0.9
Total	**117**	**100.0**

Source:- Field Survey, 2017-18.

Along with the right to education, the safety of children should also be considered an extremely important aspect. About the time children go to school, come home from there, and sit in school, it is important to address the concerns of parents in terms of security. In Table 6.5 we can see that most of the parents believe that they do not consider the system of schools neither very good nor very bad in this regard or neither agree nor disagree (47.9%) with the transportation system followed by agree (35%), while only 0.9% of the parents were found very satisfied in this context.

Table 6.6: Environment Supports Learning

	Frequency	Percentage
Not at all familiar	11	9.4
Slightly familiar	31	26.5
Somewhat familiar	42	35.9
Moderately familiar	17	14.5
Extremely familiar	16	13.7
Total	**117**	**100.0**

Source:- Field Survey, 2017-18.

As evident from Table 6.6, the majority of the parents think that their child's school environment is somewhat familiar (35.9%) followed by slightly familiar (26.5%), where only 13.7% of parents think their child's school environment is extremely familiar. It will be very helpful to see Figure 6.4 to understand the learning environment of their school.

Figure 6.4: Schools' Environment Supports Learning (in Percentage).

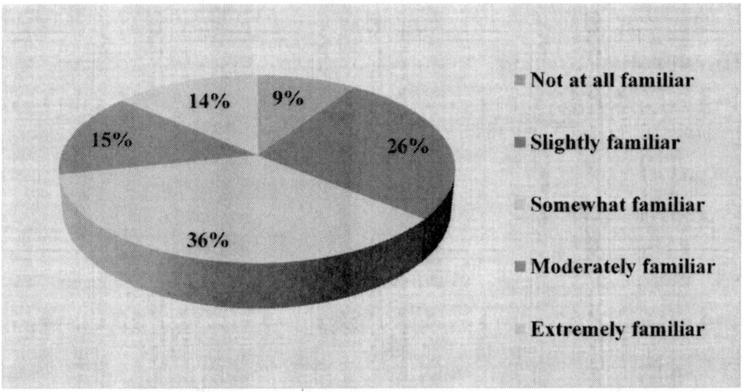

Table 6.7: Parents' Income and Type of School

Income	Type of School			Total
	Government	Private aided	Private unaided	
0-50 k	13(11.1%)	0(0.0%)	11(9.4%)	24(20.5%)
50 k-1 lac	27(23.1%)	2(1.7%)	3 (2.6%)	32(27.4%)
1-2 lac	0 (0.0%)	4(3.4%)	11(9.4%)	15(12.8%)
2-5 lac	1(0.9%)	6(5.1%)	38(32.5%)	45(38.5%)
5 and above	0(0.0%)	0(0.0%)	1(0.9%)	1(0.9%)
Total	**41(35.0%)**	**12(10.3%)**	**64(54.7%)**	**117(100.0%)**

Source:- Field Survey, 2017-18.

It is generally seen that people from different levels of society get their children enrolled in schools of that level. In the current study, an attempt was made to know from parents about their income and admission of their children and this has been displayed in Table 6.7. We can see that parent with incomes above 2 lakhs have enrolled their children in private schools (32.5%) rather than government schools. Whereas parents with an annual income of 50 thousand to 1 lakh have enrolled their children in the government schools (23.1%). This makes one thing more understandable; parents with less than 2 lakh annual income are unable to get their children admitted to private schools. And if we add parents with income from 0 to 1 lakh, it is about 34.2%. It means, that only low-income parents enroll their children in government schools, whereas it is necessary to provide equal education to people of different strata of society.

C. Acceptability

Table 6.8: Sensitive to issues regarding Race, Gender, Sexual Orientation, and Disabilities

	Frequency	Percentage
Not a priority	38	32.5
Low priority	34	29.1
Medium priority	35	29.9
High priority	9	7.7
Essential	1	0.9
Total	**117**	**100.0**

Source:- Field Survey, 2017-18.

Figure 6.5: Sensitivity in Schools Regarding Different Students.

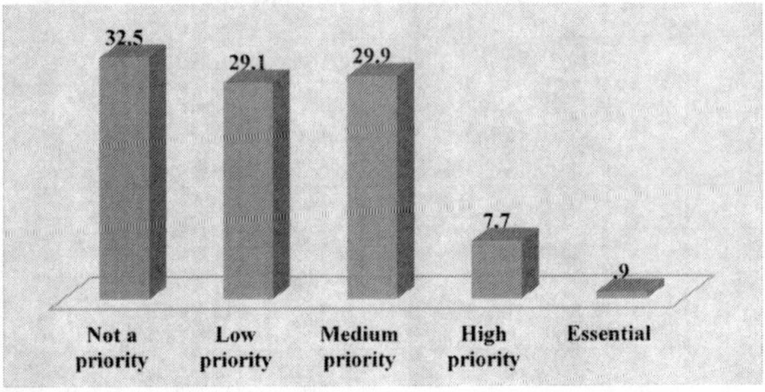

One of the most important aspects of the right to education is the sensitivity of people related to education is seen from the point of view of different types of children like caste, gender, region inability, etc. In Table 6.8 we can see, that efforts were made by the author to find out what the parents believe in this regard. It has been assumed by most of the professionals that the attitude of people related to education is not acceptable (32.5%). While 7.7% of the parents considered the schools to be good in this regard, this can be easily understood by Figure 6.5.

Table 6.9: Types of School and Sensitivity

Type of School	Sensitive to issues regarding race, gender, sexual orientation and disabilities					Total
	Not a priority	Low priority	Medium priority	High priority	Essential	
Government	13(11.1%)	20(17.1%)	8(6.8%)	0(0.0%)	0(0.0%)	41(35.0%)
Private aided	2(1.7%)	0(0.0%)	4(3.4%)	5(4.3%)	1(0.9%)	12(10.3%)
Private unaided	23(19.7%)	14(12.0%)	23(19.7%)	4(3.4%)	0(0.0%)	64(54.7%)
Total	**38(32.5%)**	**34(29.1%)**	**35(29.9%)**	**9(7.7%)**	**1(0.9%)**	**117(100.0%)**

Source:- Field Survey, 2017-18.

Under the Right to Education Act, it has been said to provide free and compulsory education to all children. In this regard, during the present survey, attempts were made to know from parents of primary school children about the attitude of teachers and administrators of various schools. We can understand their answers through Table 6.9. We can see that about 19.7% of parents believe that their children have medium priority in private unaided schools and there is no discrimination, whereas only 6.8% of the parents have the feeling that their children get medium priority in government schools.

Table 6.10: Environments of Schools and Behaviour of Teachers and Administrators

Environment supports learning	Behaviour of the teachers and administrators					Total
	Inappro-priate	Slightly inappro-priate	Neutral	Slightly appro-priate	Appro-priate	
Not at all familiar	4(3.4%)	5(4.3%)	2(1.7%)	0(0.0%)	0(0.0%)	11(9.4%)
Slightly familiar	7(6.0%)	9(7.7%)	13(11.1%)	2(1.7%)	0(0.0%)	31(26.5%)
Somewhat familiar	4(3.4%)	10(8.5%)	20(17.1%)	5(4.3%)	3(2.6%)	42(35.9%)
Moderately familiar	2(1.7%)	5(4.3%)	9(7.7%)	1(0.9%)	0(0.0%)	17(14.5%)
Extremely familiar	0(0.0%)	7(6.0%)	6(5.1%)	3(2.6%)	0(0.0%)	16(13.7%)
Total	**17(14.5%)**	**36(30.8%)**	**50(42.7%)**	**11(9.4%)**	**3(2.6%)**	**117(100.0%)**

Source:- Field Survey, 2017-18.

To increase primary education, there is a need to make the school environment conducive to children's reading and learning along with teachers and administrators should also treat children and their parents well. Through Table 6.10, an attempt can be made to understand the views of parents in this regard. We can see that only 17.1% of the parents have observed that the school environment supports learning and the behaviour of teachers and administrators are neutral. While 3.4% of the respondents or parents have accepted that the school attitude is inappropriate and not at all familiar in both these cases.

D. Adaptability

Table 6.11: Satisfied with the Opportunity to be Involved in Decisions

	Frequency	Percentage
Not at all satisfied	9	7.7
Slightly satisfied	17	14.5
Moderately satisfied	66	56.4
Very satisfied	20	17.1
Extremely satisfied	5	4.3
Total	**117**	**100.0**

Source:- Field Survey, 2017-18.

Figure 6.6: Parent's Satisfaction with Opportunity in Decisions.

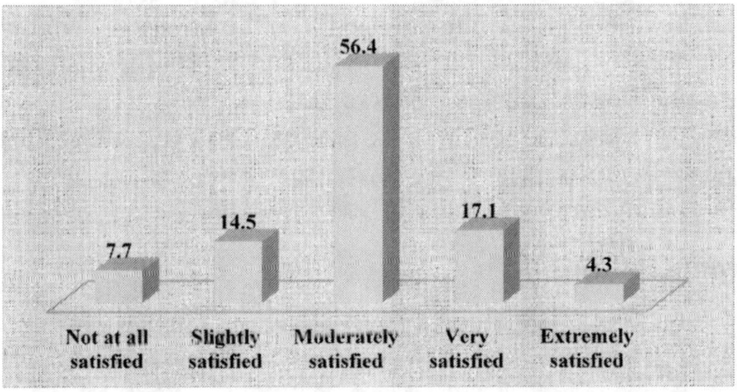

Table 6.11 shows parents' opportunities to be involved in school decisions. The majority of the parents believe that they are moderately satisfied (56.4%) with the opportunities to be involved in school decisions, whereas only 4.3% of parents believe that they are extremely satisfied with the opportunities of involvement in school decisions, which have also been attempted to understand through Figure 6.6.

Table 6.12: Satisfied with Their Input into Decisions

	Frequency	Percentage
Much worse	6	5.1
Somewhat worse	39	33.3
About the same	40	34.2
Somewhat better	22	18.8
Much better	10	8.5
Total	**117**	**100.0**

Source:- Field Survey, 2017-18.

Figure 6.7: Parents' Satisfaction with Their Inputs in School's Decision.

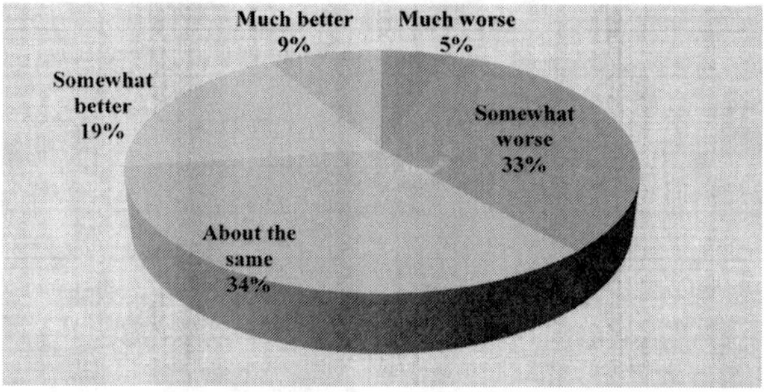

Involvement in decisions can be a reason for parental satisfaction but more important than this is how many of the parents' decisions were approved. Table 6.12 shows the satisfaction of the parents with the decisions accepted given by them. In this we can see that, most of the parents believe that the attitude of the schools in this regard is neither very good nor bad or about the same (34.2%) followed by parents who believe that the attitude of the schools in this regard is somewhat worse (33.3%), which we can easily understand through Figure 6.7.

E. Accountability

Table 6.13: Behaviour of the Teachers and Administrators

	Frequency	Percentage
Inappropriate	17	14.5
Slightly inappropriate	36	30.8
Neutral	50	42.7
Slightly appropriate	11	9.4
Appropriate	3	2.6
Total	**117**	**100.0**

Source:- Field Survey, 2017-18.

Figure 6.8: Behaviour of the Teachers and Administrators.

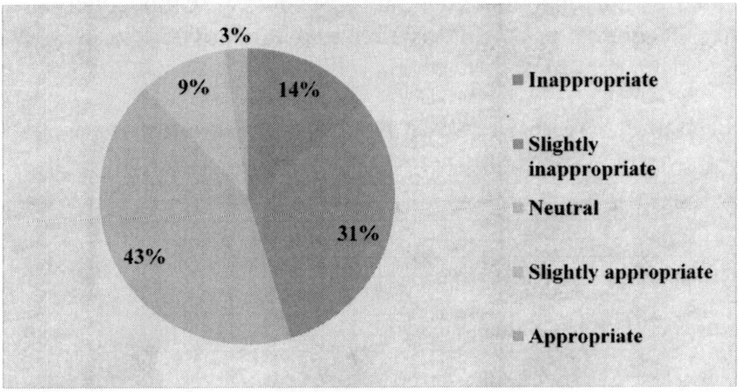

Proper behaviour or decency of the teachers and administrators is very necessary to remove the fear of children and the inhibitions of their parents. Due to which, unprecedented development can also be made in the education of children. Regarding the behaviour of teachers and administrators, an effort was made to get their opinions from parents during the survey. In Table 6.13, we can see that parents believe that the behaviour of teachers and administrators in this regard is neutral (42.7%), whereas only 2.6% of parents believe that the behaviour of teachers and administrators is very good or appropriate, which we can easily understand through Figure 6.8.

Table 6.14: Types of School and Parents' Opportunity in Decisions

Type of Schools	Satisfaction with the opportunity in school decisions					Total
	Not at all satisfied	Slightly satisfied	Moderately satisfied	Very satisfied	Extremely satisfied	
Government	3(2.6%)	8(6.8%)	30(25.6%)	0(0.0%)	0(0.0%)	41(35.0%)
Private aided	2(1.7%)	2(1.7%)	2(1.7%)	5(4.3%)	1(0.9%)	12(10.3%)
Private unaided	4(3.4%)	7(6.0%)	34(29.1%)	15(12.8%)	4(3.4%)	64(54.7%)
Total	**9(7.7%)**	**17(14.5%)**	**66(56.4%)**	**20(17.1%)**	**5(4.3%)**	**117(100.0%)**

Source:- Field Survey, 2017-18.

Teachers and administrators are also responsive to how much they involve parents in meetings related to primary education. During the survey, the author tried to know the parents' views in this regard. This can be understood through Table 6.14. About 29.1% of the parents were moderately satisfied with private schools and about 12.8% were very satisfied with private schools, which is 41.9% when added together. While only 25.6% of parents from government schools were moderately satisfied. During the survey, not a single parent was found who was very satisfied with these matters from government schools.

Table 6.15: Teacher(s)/School Tells Child's Academic Performance

	Frequency	Percentage
Never	3	2.6
Rarely	35	29.9
Occasionally	46	39.3
A moderate amount	24	20.5
A great deal	9	7.7
Total	**117**	**100.0**

Source:- Field Survey, 2017-18.

At present it is necessary to see that regarding the performance of children, whether or not informed to the parents from time to time by academic officers and teachers. It also shows the accountability of related administrators and teachers regarding education. The response given by the parents in this regard is shown in Table 6.15. In this we can see that, most of the parents believe that they are told by the school occasionally or somewhat familiar (39.3%), while 2.6% of the parents believe that they are never informed in this regard, this can be easily understood by Figure 6.9.

Figure 6.9: Teacher(s)/Schools Tells Child's Academic Performance.

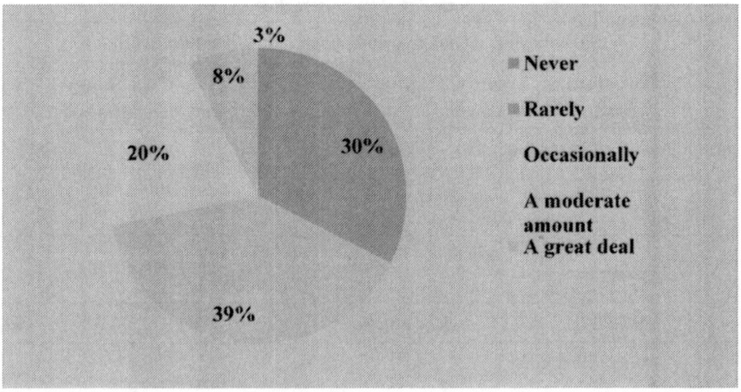

6.3. Demographic and Academic Profile of the Teachers and Administrators

Table 6.16 shows the introductory demographic and socio-economic profile of the teachers and administrators of the primary schools surveyed using schedule questionnaire. A total of 234 teachers and administrators were interviewed during the primary survey, which included 140 (59.82%) male respondents and 94 (40.17%) female respondents, which can be easily understood in Figure 6.10. The task of selecting 234 teachers and administrators was done through the Taro Yamane formula, i.e. $n = N/\{1+N(e^2)\}$. The total number of private, private aided and government schools under the Varanasi Municipal Corporation is 166(NIEPA, n.d.). In Table 6.16, we can see that most of these individuals are from teaching backgrounds (65.4%) followed by administrators (34.6%). During the survey, the author got to know about the qualifications of the respondents, where 51 (21.8%) respondents was graduates and/or B.Ed. and 183 (78.2%) respondents were postgraduate and above. The areas covered during the primary survey were urban (38.5%) and semi-urban (61.5%). Schools can be seen as government (21.8%), private aided (15.4%), and private unaided (62.8%).

Table 6.16: Introductory Characteristics of Teachers and Administrators of Schools

Demographic Profile	Parameters	Number of Participants	Percentage of Participants
Gender	*Male*	140	59.82
	Female	94	40.17
	Total	**234**	**100**
Designation	*Teachers*	153	65.4
	Administrators	81	34.6
	Total	**234**	**100**
Qualification	*Graduates*	51	21.8
	Post-Graduates and Above	183	78.2
	Total	**234**	**100**
Location	*Urban*	90	38.5
	Semi-urban	144	61.5
	Total	**234**	**100**
Type of School	*Government*	51	21.8
	Private-aided	36	15.4
	Private-unaided	147	62.8
	Total	**234**	**100**

Source:- Field Survey, 2017-18.

Figure 6.10: Genders of Teachers and Administrators.

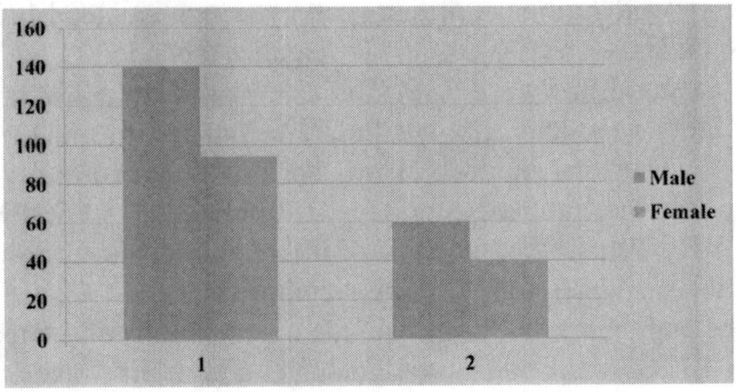

6.4. Teachers and Administrators' Views and Attitudes towards various Indicators of 4As and Accountability

In this section of data analysis, an attempt has been made to analyze the attitude of teachers and administrators towards the 4A scheme and awareness about the accountability of different aspects of the RTE Act in the city of Varanasi through numerous tables and appropriate figures and graphs.

A. Availability

Table 6.17: Procedure for Admission of Students in Schools

	Frequency	Percentage
Personal Interview	66	28.2
Written Test	48	20.5
Oral Test	50	21.4
Both written and oral test	64	27.4
Any other	6	2.6
Total	**234**	**100.0**

Source:- Field Survey, 2017-18.

Under the Right to Education Act, education of aged 6-14 years is considered free and compulsory. During the survey, it was important to know the admission process of children in various government and private schools. In this regard, an attempt was made to know the views of teachers and administrators associated with elementary education, which can be understood through Table 6.17. We can see that, most of the teachers and administrators say that the admission process is usually run through personal interviews (28.2%), followed by teachers and administrators who answered that the admission process is going through both written and oral tests (27.4%).

Table 6.18: Availability of Teachers

	Frequency	Percentage
Insufficient	22	9.4
Somewhat insufficient	93	39.7
Neither insufficient nor sufficient	86	36.8
Somewhat sufficient	9	3.8
Sufficient	24	10.3
Total	**234**	**100.0**

Source:- Field Survey, 2017-18.

Figure 6.11: Availability of Teachers.

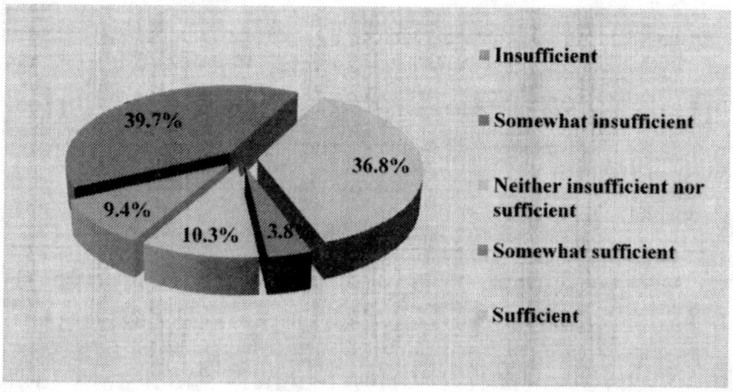

A lack of teachers is commonly seen in elementary schools at various times. Under the Right to Education Act, it is provisioned that students and teacher ratio should be 30:1. In this regard, an attempt was made to know the status of various schools from teachers and administrators, which can be understood through Table 6.18. We can see that about 39.7% of teachers and teachers believe that there is somewhat insufficient or a shortage of teachers in schools followed by 36.8% of teachers and teachers, who think that the status regarding teachers' availability is neither insufficient nor sufficient. This can be understood in Figure 6.11.

Table 6.19: Adequate Playgrounds and Open Spaces for Recreation

	Frequency	Percentage
Insufficient	21	9.0
Somewhat insufficient	9	3.8
Neither insufficient nor sufficient	36	15.4
Somewhat sufficient	92	39.3
Sufficient	76	32.5
Total	**234**	**100.0**

Source:- Field Survey, 2017-18.

Sports are very important for children because it helps children to increase their physical benefits as well as their mental capacity. For this, special provisions have been made about the place or area for sports in various schools under the Right to Education Act. In this regard, information was obtained from various teachers and administrators related to elementary education, as shown in Table 6.19. We can see that most of the teachers and administrators believe that places for sports in various schools are somewhat sufficient (39.3%), followed by teachers and administrators who believe it is as sufficient (32.5%).

Table 6.20: Facilities for Medical Check-ups

	Frequency	Percentage
Inappropriate	24	10.3
Slightly inappropriate	34	14.5
Neutral	52	22.2
Slightly appropriate	54	23.1
Appropriate	70	29.9
Total	**234**	**100.0**

Source:- Field Survey, 2017-18.

Information was also received from teachers and administrators about the necessary items and treatment in schools, which is very important for children. An attempt has been made to explain this through Table 6.20. We can see that most of the teachers and administrators believe that it is appropriate (29.9%) in various schools. Followed by teachers and administrators who believe it is slightly appropriate (23.1%).

Table 6.21: Not Available Facilities

	Frequency	Percentage
Office Room	9	3.8
Urinal and Lavatories	42	17.9
Drinking water	5	2.1
Library	58	24.8
Any Other	120	51.3
Total	**234**	**100.0**

Source:- Field Survey, 2017-18.

Figure 6.12: Not Available Facilities.

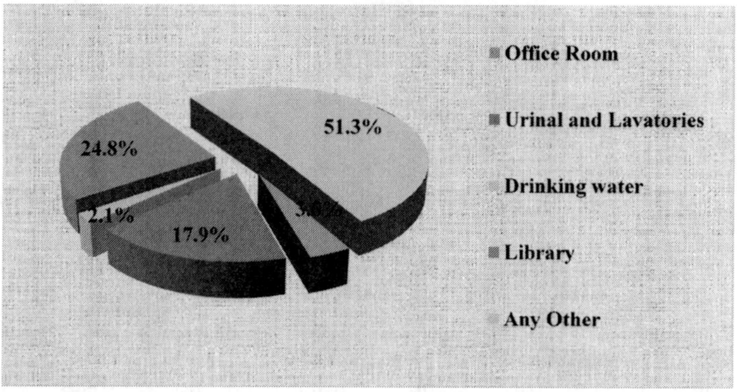

Information was received from teachers and administrators regarding the availability and maintenance of different types of facilities in various schools, which we can see in Table 6.21. In this regard, respondents believe that all facilities are generally available, but under any others (51.3%) we can include some things, which we miss sometimes like different types of learning material, etc., followed by lack of library (24.8%). Regarding maintenance of various facilities, the urinals and lavatories (17.9%) should be cleaned. This can be easily understood through Figure 6.12.

B. Affordability

Table 6.22: Education Affordable to All

	Frequency	Percentage
Strongly disagree	9	3.8
Disagree	24	10.3
Neither agree or disagree	106	45.3
Agree	80	34.2
Strongly agree	15	6.4
Total	**234**	**100.0**

Source:- Field Survey, 2017-18.

Figure 6.13: Education Affordable to All.

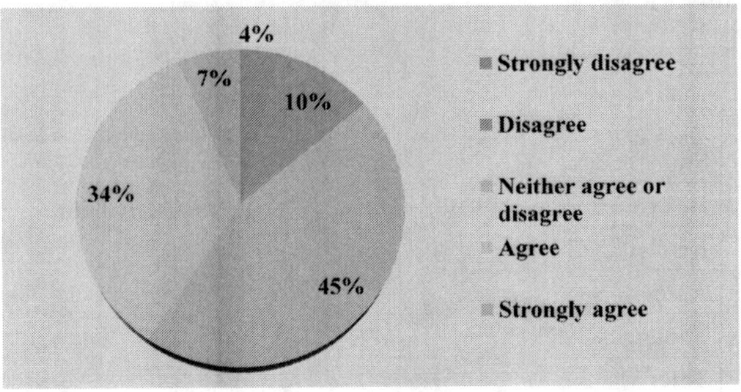

Under the Right to Education Act, it has been said to provide free and compulsory education to all children. In this regard, during the present survey, attempts were made to know from the teachers and administrators of the primary school about the affordability of education. Through Table 6.22, we can know the views of teachers and administrators about it. We can see that 45.3% of teachers and administrators believe that they neither agree nor disagree in this regard. Subsequently, 34.2% of teachers and administrators believe that elementary education is affordable to their children, which we can easily understand through Figure 6.13.

Table 6.23: Any Hostel or Boarding for Students

	Frequency	Percentage
Strongly disagree	115	49.1
Disagree	63	26.9
Neither agree or disagree	12	5.1
Agree	15	6.4
Strongly agree	29	12.4
Total	**234**	**100.0**

Source:- Field Survey, 2017-18.

It is generally observed that primary schools do not have hostels or accommodation. To know the status of various schools in Varanasi city in this regard, the present study, attempts were made to find out the answers of the teachers and administrators regarding hostels and accommodation. The author has attempted to explain this through Table 6.23. We can see that 49.1% of teachers and administrators strongly disagree or believe that there is no hostel related to their schools. Along with 26.9% of the teachers and administrators were disagreeing and believed that there are no hostels related to their schools. If we add these two numbers, we find that about 76% of the schools do not have hostels.

Table 6.24: Education within Safe Physical Reach

	Frequency	Percentage
Strongly disagree	5	2.1
Disagree	21	9.0
Neither agree or disagree	38	16.2
Agree	103	44.0
Strongly agree	67	28.6
Total	**234**	**100.0**

Source:- Field Survey, 2017-18.

Along with the right to education, the safety of children should also be considered an extremely important aspect. Concerning the time children go to school, come home from there, and sit in school, it is important to address parents' concerns regarding security. Regarding safe access to schools, the author tried to know about the views of teachers and administrators, which can be understood through Table 6.24. About 44% of teachers and administrators agreed and believe that children have safe access to schools. At the same time, about 9% of teachers and administrators disagreed in this regard and believed that children face some problems in this regard followed by 2.1% of teachers and administrators who strongly disagreed in this regard.

Table 6.25: Types of School and Education Accessible to All

Types of School	Education accessible to all					
	Strongly disagree	Disagree	Neither agree or disagree	Agree	Strongly agree	Total
Government	2(0.9%)	5(2.1%)	5(2.1%)	18(7.7%)	21(9.0%)	51(21.8%)
Private aided	1(0.4%)	4(1.7%)	5(2.1%)	9(3.8%)	17(7.3%)	36(15.4%)
Private unaided	6(2.6%)	15(6.4%)	5(2.1%)	53(22.6%)	68(29.1%)	147(62.8%)
Total	**9(3.8%)**	**24(10.3%)**	**15(6.4%)**	**80(34.2%)**	**106(45.3%)**	**234(100.0%)**

Source:- Field Survey, 2017-18.

Under the Right to Education Act, provisions have been made for free and compulsory education to all 6-14-year-olds. In the current study, efforts were made to know from the teachers and administrators how they see these provisions from the point of view of reality, which is shown in Table 6.25.

We can see that, out of a total of 21.8% surveyed government elementary education teachers and administrators, about 9% of the respondents strongly agreed and believed that all children have access to elementary education, followed by 7.7% of teachers and administrators who agreed and believed that all children have access to primary education.

Whereas out of a total of 15.4% of respondents (teachers and administrators) of private aided schools, about 7.3% of the respondents strongly agreed that all children have access to elementary education, followed by 3.8% of teachers and administrators who agreed believed that all children have access to primary education.

And out of the total 62.8% of respondents or teachers and administrators related to private schools, only 29.1% of them strongly agreed that all children have access to elementary education, followed by 22.6% of teachers and administrators who agreed and believed that all children have access to education. In this way, about 79.5% of the total 100% of respondents agreed or strongly agreed that all children have access to elementary education. Whereas 14.1% of the respondents are those who disagreed or strongly disagreed that all children have access to elementary education. At the same time, about 6.4% of respondents neither agree nor disagree that all children have access to elementary education.

C. Acceptability

Table 6.26: Well-Trained Teacher

	Frequency	**Percentage**
Strongly disagree	31	13.2
Disagree	39	16.7
Neither agree or disagree	51	21.8
Agree	48	20.5
Strongly agree	65	27.8
Total	**234**	**100.0**

Source:- Field Survey, 2017-18.

In the present study, attempts were made to get information from teachers and administrators regarding their training, which is presented under Table 6.26. We can see that most of the teachers and administrators strongly agree (27.8%) that the system of training in elementary education is good, followed by teachers and administrators who agreed (20.5%) and believed that it is something good. But from the perspective of all the respondents, this number is not even 50%. Due to the lack of training of teachers and administrators, children do not get proper education. Because of this, there is a possibility of children dropping out of school. Fixing this problem is currently very important.

Table 6.27: Have Appropriate Working Conditions, Teaching Material, and the Right to Organise

	Frequency	Percentage
Not at all influential	13	5.6
Slightly influential	36	15.4
Somewhat influential	66	28.2
Very influential	86	36.8
Extremely influential	33	14.1
Total	**234**	**100.0**

Source:- Field Survey, 2017-18.

Administrative decentralisation is very important for increasing primary education level and can be achieved through the appropriate working conditions, teaching material the right to organise in schools. In this regard, an effort was made to get information from various teachers and administrators regarding their efficacy, which can be understood through Table 6.27. We can see that, most of the teachers and administrators believe that the present training system is very influential in this regard (36.8%), followed by teachers and administrators who believe it is somewhat influential (28.2%).

Table 6.28: Present Method of Recruitment of Teachers

	Frequency	Percentage
Not at all satisfied	14	6.0
Slightly satisfied	44	18.8
Moderately satisfied	55	23.5
Very satisfied	106	45.3
Extremely satisfied	15	6.4
Total	**234**	**100.0**

Source:- Field Survey, 2017-18.

The present study also asked teachers and administrators about their satisfaction with the recruitment process of teachers in elementary schools. As shown in Table 6.28, we can see that most of the teachers and administrators believe that they are very satisfied (45.3%) with the current recruitment process, followed by teachers and administrators who were moderately satisfied (23.5%) with the current recruitment process.

Table 6.29: Types of School and Well-Trained Teacher

Type of School	Well trained teacher					Total
	Strongly disagree	Disagree	Neither agree or disagree	Agree	Strongly agree	
Government	7(3.0%)	6(2.6%)	7(3.0%)	10(4.3%)	21(9.0%)	51(21.8%)
Private aided	3(1.3%)	4(1.7%)	7(3.0%)	9(3.8%)	13(5.6%)	36(15.4%)
Private unaided	21(9.0%)	29(12.4%)	37(15.8%)	29(12.4%)	31(13.2%)	147(62.8%)
Total	**31(13.2%)**	**39(16.7%)**	**51(21.8%)**	**48(20.5%)**	**65(27.8%)**	**234(100.0%)**

Source:- Field Survey, 2017-18.

Efforts were made to know about the access to training and satisfaction of teachers and administrators of various governments, private aided and private unaided schools, which is shown under Table 6.29. We can see that about 9% of the teachers and administrators strongly agreed that they have access to training, followed by 4.3% of teachers and administrators who agreed about it.

About 5.6% of private aided teachers and administrators are strongly agreed that they have access to training, followed by 3.8% of the teachers and administrators who agreed about it. At the same time, about 15.8% of the teachers and administrators belonging to private schools neither agree nor disagree that they have access to training, followed by 13.2% of the teachers and administrators who strongly agreed that they have access to training and 12.4% of the teachers and administrators agreed about it. Out of 100% of respondents, about 16.7% of them disagreed about their access to training, followed by teachers and administrators who strongly disagreed (13.2%) about their access to training.

D. Adaptability

Table 6.30: Parents consult regarding the Education of their Children

	Frequency	Percentage
Not at all concerned	24	10.3
Slightly concerned	21	9.0
Somewhat concerned	27	11.5
Moderately concerned	102	43.6
Extremely concerned	60	25.6
Total	**234**	**100.0**

Source:- Field Survey, 2017-18.

Figure 6.14: Parents consult regarding the Education of their Children.

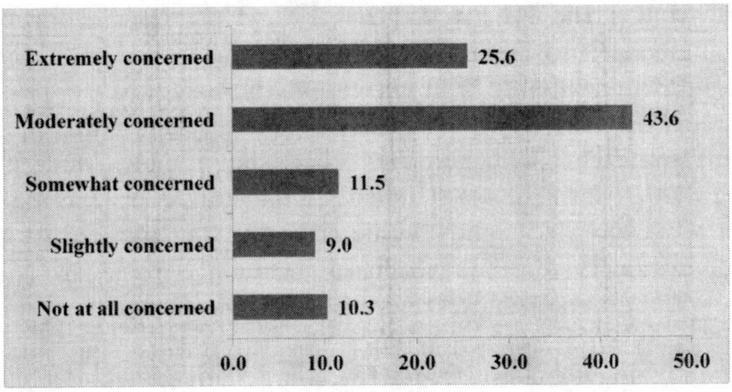

Information was also obtained from teachers and administrators about whether or not parents meet or consult teachers and administrators from time to time for their children's education, which is shown in Table 6.30. Most of the teachers and administrators believe that parents are moderately concerned (43.6%) in this regard, followed by teachers and administrators who say parents are extremely concerned (25.6%) which can be understood in Figure 6.14.

E. Accountability

Table 6.31: Parent-Teacher Associations

	Frequency	Percentage
Not at all influential	9	3.8
Slightly influential	94	40.2
Somewhat influential	68	29.1
Very influential	63	26.9
Total	**234**	**100.0**

Source:- Field Survey, 2017-18.

Figure 6.15: Parent-Teacher Associations.

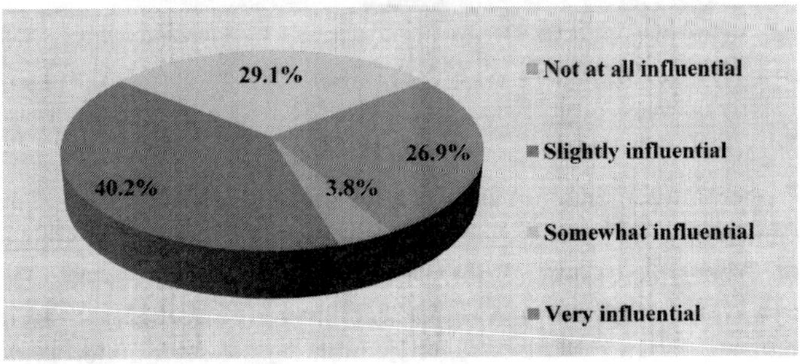

An important means of increasing elementary education is to have periodic conversations between teachers and parents and meet for the same. Important provisions have also been made in this regard under the Right to Education Act. In current study, during the primary survey, efforts were made to know the views of various teachers and administrators about parent-teacher association which is shown under Table 6.31. We can see that most of the teachers and administrators believe that parent-teacher association is slightly influential (40.2%), followed by teachers and administrators who believe that association is somewhat influential (29.1%). We can easily understand this through Figure 6.15.

Table 6.32: Inspector of School Visits School

	Frequency	Percentage
Never	15	6.4
Rarely	51	21.8
Sometimes	86	36.8
Often	48	20.5
Always	34	14.5
Total	**234**	**100.0**

Source:- Field Survey, 2017-18.

Figure 6.16: Inspector of School Visits School.

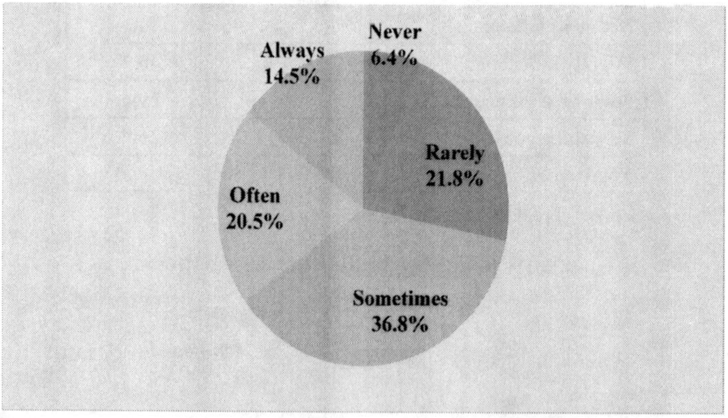

Proper implementation of the Right to Education Act also depends on whether inspectors associated with elementary education visit various schools from time to time or not. During the primary survey, an effort was made to know the views of various teachers and administrators related to elementary education, in this regard which can be seen under Table 6.32.

Most of the teachers and administrators believe that inspectors sometimes (36.8%) visit schools, followed by teachers and administrator who believe inspectors rarely (21.8%) visit school. About 6.4% of teachers also felt that inspectors do not visit schools at all. We can understand this easily with the help of Figure 6.16.

Table 6.33: School Inspected Last

	Frequency	Percentage
12-24 months ago	27	11.5
9-12 months ago	93	39.7
6-9 months ago	74	31.6
3-6 months ago	24	10.3
0-3 months ago	16	6.8
Total	**234**	**100.0**

Source:- Field Survey, 2017-18.

Figure 6.17: School Inspected Last.

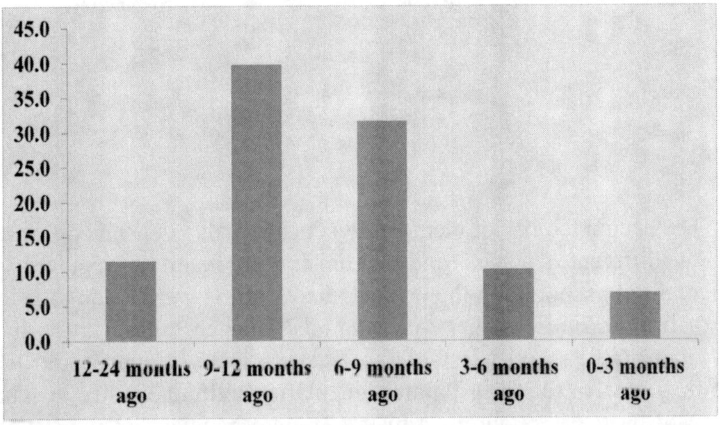

The accountability of the inspector of schools also depends on how often in a month or year he visits the schools. Information was obtained from various government and private aided and private unaided teachers and administrators in this regard, which is shown under Table 6.33. We can see that, most of the teachers and administrators believed that inspectors of schools were inspected lastly 9-12 months (39.7%) ago, followed by teachers and administrators who felt that inspectors visited schools 6-9 months (31.6%) ago, which can be understood through Figure 6.17.

Table 6.34: Maintenance of Regularity and Punctuality

	Frequency	Percentage
Never	15	6.4
Rarely	21	9.0
Sometimes	63	26.9
Often	51	21.8
Always	84	35.9
Total	**234**	**100.0**

Source:- Field Survey, 2017-18.

Figure 6.18: Maintenance of Regularity and Punctuality.

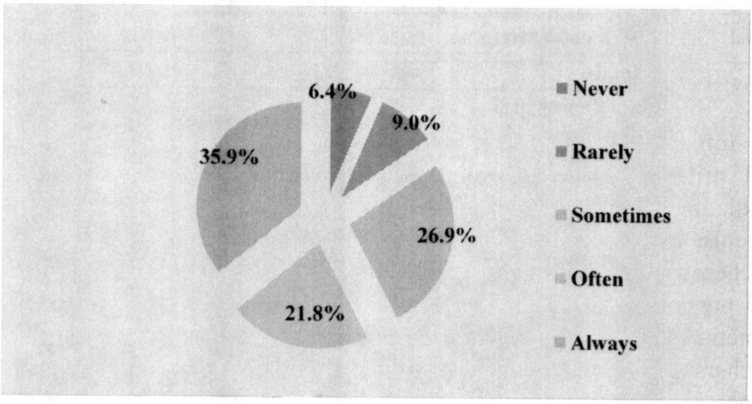

The accountability of elementary education also depends on, whether or not different teachers and administrators maintain regularity and punctuality in schools. In the present study, efforts were made to get their views from various teachers and administrators in this regard, which is shown in Table 6.34. Most of the teachers and administrators believe that they always (35.9%) maintain regularity and punctuality in schools, followed by teachers and administrators who believe that they maintain regularity and punctuality sometimes (26.9%), which can be understood through Figure 6.18.

Table 6.35: Maintenance of Regularity and Punctuality and Inspector of School Visit Schools

Maintenance of Regularity and Punctuality	The inspector of the school visits the school					Total
	Never	Rarely	Sometimes	Often	Always	
Never	0(0.0%)	7(3.0%)	3(1.3%)	2(0.9%)	3(1.3%)	15(6.4%)
Rarely	2(0.9%)	3(1.3%)	11(4.7%)	4(1.7%)	1(0.4%)	21(9.0%)
Sometimes	3(1.3%)	15(6.4%)	22(9.4%)	15(6.4%)	8(3.4%)	63(26.9%)
Often	6(2.6%)	10(4.3%)	15(6.4%)	11(4.7%)	9(3.8%)	51(21.8%)
Always	4(1.7%)	16(6.8%)	35(15.0%)	16(6.8%)	13(5.6%)	84(35.9%)
Total	**15(6.4%)**	**51(21.8%)**	**86(36.8%)**	**48(20.5%)**	**34(14.5%)**	**234(100.0%)**

Source:- Field Survey, 2017-18.

Information was received by various government, private aided, and private unaided schools' teachers and administrators regarding regulations and punctuality of themselves and visits of the inspector of schools, which is shown under Table 6.35. We can see that, most of the teachers and administrators felt that they always (15%) maintain regularity and punctuality in schools and the inspector of the school visits school sometimes. Only 5.6% of teachers and administrators believe and feel that teachers and administrators always maintain regularity and punctuality and inspectors of schools visit schools.

6.5. Limitations of this Empirical Study

This empirical study has been limited to the urban and semi-urban areas of the Varanasi district. A very significant limitation of this empirical study has been the fact that the concept of accountability of administration was rather new to a lot of the teachers and administrators of the primary schools. This is also visible in a high percentage of respondents who were undecided on several questions related to accountability. It is nevertheless the attempt has been made that the reliability and validity of the empirical study have not been compromised since the study did not delve deeper into the intricacies of accountability but only into the aspects that were relevant to this study in the city of Varanasi.

Summary of Findings and Recommendations

Chapter - VII

Summary of Findings and Recommendations

This chapter aims to examine the research objectives of the book like: (a) To conceptualise access i.e., examine the main constituents of access to primary education, (b) To develop suitable indicators of availability, affordability, acceptability, and adaptability, (c) To identify the indicators (among 4A's) which are responsible for low access in the Varanasi district of Uttar Pradesh, (d) To identify the possibilities of an accountable educational administration.

7.1. Major Findings

In this section findings of the study have been discussed.

7.1.1. Demographic and Socio-Economic Profile of Parents of Varanasi

- According to the 2011 census, the population of Varanasi district is 3682194. Varanasi's rank in terms of population is 18th in the state of Uttar Pradesh. The urban population of Varanasi district is 1597051, which is 43.4%, while in the state of Uttar Pradesh; the percentage of urban population is about 22.3. The population density of the Varanasi district is 2395 persons per Sq. /Km. which is much higher than the population density of Uttar Pradesh i.e. 829 persons per sq.km.
- In the city the majority of the respondents (62.39%) were men and only 37.60% of respondents were women.
- Most of the parents have an income of Rs 1 lakh to 2 lakh (38.5%) annually followed by parents with Rs 50 thousand to 1 lakh (27.4%).

- It has the highest number of self-employed people (29.9%) which is followed by the number of parents associated with other work (19.7%) and agriculture (17.9%).
- The areas covered during the primary survey were urban (62.4%) and semi-urban (37.6%).

7.1.2. Parent's Views and Attitudes towards various indicators of 4As and Accountability

Findings related to the attitude of parents towards the 4A scheme and awareness about the accountability of different aspects of the RTE Act in the city of Varanasi.

1. **Availability**
   - The majority of the parents (35%) are moderately satisfied with the primary education of their children followed by parents (34.2%) who think that they are slightly satisfied with the primary education system of Varanasi. Only 6% of parents are satisfied with the quality of their child's education.
   - Most of the parents think that the opportunities to participate in the physical education of their child's school are somewhat influential (39.3%) followed by slightly influential (30.8%).
   - Along with the resources available in schools, its cleanliness and maintenance are also an important issue. In this regard, it was seen at various times that, many children leave schools just because the toilets, tables, chairs, etc., are not kept clean. In this regard, efforts were made to know the views of the parents. Most of the parents are neither very concerned nor very happy in this regard (35%). After this, 32.5% of the parents considered the schools to be good in this regard.
2. **Affordability**
   - Along with the right to education, the safety of children should also be considered an extremely important aspect. About the time children go to school, come home from there, and sit in school, it is important to address the concerns of parents in terms of security. Most of the parents believe that they do not consider the system of schools neither very good nor very bad in this regard or neither agree nor disagree (47.9%) with the transportation system followed by agree (35%), while only 0.9% the parents were found very satisfied in this context.

- The majority of the parents think that their child's school environment is somewhat familiar (35.9%) followed by slightly familiar (26.5%), where only 13.7% of parents think their child's school environment is extremely familiar.
- It is generally seen that people from different levels of society get their children enrolled in schools of that level. In the current study, an attempt was made to learn from parents about their income and the admission of their children. Parents with incomes above 2 lakhs have enrolled their children in private schools (32.5%) rather than government schools. Whereas parents with an annual income of 50 thousand to 1 lakh have enrolled their children in the government schools (23.1%). This makes one thing more understandable; parents with less than 2 lakh annual income are unable to get their children admitted to private schools. And if we add parents with income from 0 to 1 lakh, it is about 34.2%. It means, only low-income parents enroll their children in government schools, whereas it is necessary to provide equal education to people of different strata of society.

3. **Acceptability**

- One of the most important aspects of the right to education is the sensitivity of people related to education is seen from the point of view of different types of children like caste, gender, region or inability, etc. Efforts were made by the author to find out what the parents believe in this regard. It has been assumed by most of the professionals that the attitude of people related to education is not acceptable (32.5%). While 7.7% of the parents considered the schools to be good in this regard.
- Under the Right to Education Act, it has been said to provide free and compulsory education to all children. In this regard, during the present survey, attempts were made to know from parents of primary school children about the attitude of teachers and administrators of various schools. About 19.7% of parents believe that their children have medium priority in private unaided schools and there is no discrimination, whereas only 6.8% of the parents have the feeling that their children get medium priority in government schools.
- To increase primary education, there is a need to make the school environment conducive to children's reading and

learning along with teachers and administrators should also treat children and their parents well. An attempt can be made to understand the views of parents in this regard. Only 17.1% of the parents have observed that the school environment supports learning and the behaviour of teachers and administrators is neutral. While 3.4% of the respondents or parents have accepted that the school attitude is inappropriate and not at all familiar in both these cases.

4. Adaptability

- The majority of the parents believe that they are moderately satisfied (56.4%) with the opportunities to be involved in school decisions, whereas only 4.3% of parents believe that they are extremely satisfied with the opportunities of involved in school decisions.
- Involvement in decisions can be a reason for parental satisfaction, but more important than this is how many of the parents' decisions were approved. Most of the parents believe that the attitude of the schools in this regard is neither very good nor bad or about the same (34.2%) followed by parents who believe that the attitude of the schools in this regard is somewhat worse (33.3%).

5. Accountability

- Proper behaviour or decency of the teachers and administrators is very necessary to remove the fear of children and the inhibitions of their parents. Due to this, unprecedented development can also be made in the education of children. Regarding the behaviour of teachers and administrators, an effort was made to get their opinions from parents during the survey. Parents believe that the behaviour of teachers and administrators in this regard is neutral (42.7%), whereas only 2.6% of parents believe that the behaviour of teachers and administrators is very good or appropriate.
- Teachers and administrators are also responsive to how much they involve parents in meetings related to primary education. During the survey, the author tried to know the parents' views in this regard. About 29.1% of the parents were moderately satisfied with private schools and about 12.8% of parents were very satisfied with private schools, which is 41.9% when added together. While only 25.6% of parents from government schools were moderately satisfied. During the survey, not a

single parent was found who was very satisfied with these matters from government schools.

- At present it is necessary to see that regarding the performance of children, whether or not informed to the parents from time to time by academic officers and teachers. It also shows the accountability of related administrators and teachers regarding education. Most of the parents believe that they are told by the school occasionally or somewhat familiar (39.3%), while 2.6% of the parents believe that they are never informed in this regard.

7.1.3. Demographic and Academic Profile of the Teachers and Administrators

- A total of 234 teachers and administrators were interviewed during the primary survey, which included 140 (59.82%) male respondents and 94 (40.17%) female respondents.
- The task of selecting 234 teachers and administrators was done through the Taro Yamane formula, i.e. $n = N/\{1+N(e^2)\}$.
- Most of these respondents were from teaching backgrounds (65.4%) followed by administrators (34.6%).
- During the survey, the author got to know about the qualifications of the respondents, where 51 (21.8%) respondents were graduates and/or B.Ed., and 183 (78.2%) respondents were postgraduates and above.
- The areas covered during the primary survey were urban (38.5%) and semi-urban (61.5%).
- Schools can be seen as government (21.8%), private aided (15.4%), and private unaided (62.8%).

7.1.4. Teachers and Administrators' Views and Attitudes towards various indicators of 4As and Accountability

Findings related to the attitude of teachers and administrators towards the 4A scheme and awareness about 'accountability' of different aspects of the RTE Act in the city of Varanasi.

1. Availability

- Under the Right to Education Act, education of education aged 6-14 years is considered free and compulsory. During the survey, it was important to know the admission process of children in various government and private schools. In this regard, an attempt was made to know the views of teachers and administrators associated with elementary education. Most of the teachers and administrators indicated that the admission process primarily involves personal interviews (28.2%), while others mentioned that it includes both written and oral tests (27.4%).

- A lack of teachers is commonly seen in elementary schools at various times. Under the Right to Education Act, it is provisioned that students and teacher ratio should be 30:1. In this regard, an attempt was made to know the status of various schools from teachers and administrators. About 39.7% of teachers and administrators believe that there is somewhat insufficient or shortage of teachers in schools followed by 36.8% of teachers and administrators, who think that the status regarding teachers' availability is neither insufficient nor sufficient.
- Sports are very important for children because it helps children to increase their physical benefits as well as their mental capacity. For this, special provisions have been made about the place or area for sports in various schools under the Right to Education Act. In this regard, information was obtained from various teachers and administrators related to elementary education. Most of the teachers and administrators believe that places for sports in various schools are somewhat sufficient (39.3%), followed by teachers and administrators who believe it is as sufficient (32.5%).
- Information was also received from teachers and administrators about the necessary items and treatment in schools, which is very important for children. Most of the teachers and administrators believe that it is appropriate (29.9%) in various schools. Followed by teachers and administrators who believe it is slightly appropriate (23.1%).
- Information was received from teachers and administrators regarding the availability and maintenance of different types of facilities in various schools. In this regard, respondents believe that all facilities are generally available, but under any others (51.3%) we can include some things, that we miss sometimes like different types of learning material, etc.,

followed by lack of library (24.8%). As far as the maintenance of various facilities is concerned, the urinals and lavatories (17.9%) should be cleaned.

2. Affordability

- Under the Right to Education Act, it has been said to provide free and compulsory education to all children. In this regard, during the present survey, attempts were made to know from the teachers and administrators of the primary school about the affordability of education. 45.3% of teachers and administrators believe that they neither agree nor disagree in this regard. Subsequently, 34.2% of teachers and administrators believe that elementary education is affordable to their children.
- It is generally observed that primary schools do not have hostels or accommodation. To know the status of various schools in Varanasi city in this regard, the present study, attempts were made to find out the answers of the teachers and administrators regarding hostels and accommodation. 49.1% of teachers and administrators strongly disagreed or believed that there is no hostel related to their schools. Along with 26.9% of the teachers and administrators disagreed and believed that there are no hostels related to their schools. If we add these two numbers, we find that about 76% of the schools do not have hostels.
- Along with the right to education, the safety of children should also be considered an extremely important aspect. About the time children go to school, come home from there, and sit in school, it is important to address the concerns of parents in terms of security. Regarding safe access to schools, the author tried to know about the views of teachers and administrators. About 44% of teachers and administrators agreed and believe that children have safe access to schools. At the same time, about 9% of teachers and administrators disagreed in this regard and believed that children face some problems in this regard followed by 2.1% of teachers and administrators who strongly disagreed in this regard.
- Under the Right to Education Act, provisions have been made for free and compulsory education to all 6-14-year-olds. In the current study, efforts were made to know from the teachers and administrators how they see these provisions from the

point of view of reality. Out of the total of 21.8% surveyed government elementary education teachers and administrators, about 9% of the respondents strongly agreed and believed that all children have access to elementary education, followed by 7.7% of teachers and administrators who agreed and believed that all children have access to primary education.

- Whereas out of a total of 15.4% of respondents (teachers and administrators) of private aided schools, about 7.3% of the respondents strongly agreed that all children have access to elementary education, followed by 3.8% of teachers and administrators who agreed that all children have access to primary education.
- Out of the total 62.8% of respondents or teachers and administrators related to private schools, only 29.1% of them strongly agreed that all children have access to elementary education, followed by 22.6% of teachers and administrators who agreed and believed that all children have access to education.
- In this way, about 79.5% of the total 100% of respondents agreed or strongly agreed that all children have access to elementary education. Whereas 14.1% of the respondents are those who disagreed or strongly disagreed that all children have access to elementary education. At the same time, about 6.4% of respondents neither agree nor disagree that all children have access to elementary education.

3. Acceptability

- In the present study, attempts were made to get information from teachers and administrators regarding their training. Most of the teachers and administrators strongly agree (27.8%) that the system of training in elementary education is good, followed by teachers and administrators who agreed (20.5%) and believed that it is something good. But from the perspective of all the respondents, this number is not even 50%. Due to the lack of training of teachers and administrators, children do not get proper education. Because of this, there is a possibility of children dropping out of school. Fixing this problem is currently very important.
- Administrative decentralisation is very important for increasing primary education level and can be achieved through the appropriate working conditions, teaching

material the right to organise in schools. In this regard, an effort was made to get information from various teachers and administrators regarding their efficacy. Most of the teachers and administrators believe that the present training system is very influential in this regard (36.8%), followed by teachers and administrators who believe it is somewhat influential (28.2%).

- The present study also asked teachers and administrators about their satisfaction with the recruitment process of teachers in elementary schools. Most of the teachers and administrators believe that they are very satisfied (45.3%) with the current recruitment process, followed by teachers and administrators who were moderately satisfied (23.5%) with the current recruitment process.
- Efforts were made to know about the access to training and satisfaction of teachers and administrators of various governments, private aided and private unaided schools from themselves. About 9% of the teachers and administrators strongly agree that they have access to training, followed by 4.3% of teachers and administrators who agree.
- About 5.6% of private-aided teachers and administrators strongly agreed that they have access to training, followed by 3.8% of the teachers and administrators who agreed about it.
- At the same time, about 15.8% of the teachers and administrators belonging to private schools neither agree nor disagree that they have access to training, followed by 13.2% of the teachers and administrators who strongly agreed that they have access to training and 12.4% of the teachers and administrators agreed about it.
- Out of 100% of respondents, about 16.7% of them disagreed about their access to training, followed by teachers and administrators who strongly disagreed (13.2%) about their access to training.

4. Adaptability

- Information was also obtained from teachers and administrators about whether or not parents meet or consult teachers and administrators from time to time for their children's education. Most of the teachers and administrators believe that parents are moderately concerned (43.6%) in this regard, followed by teachers and administrators who say parents are extremely concerned (25.6%).

5. **Accountability**

- An important means of increasing elementary education is to have periodic conversations between teachers and parents and meet for the same. Important provisions have also been made in this regard under the Right to Education Act. In the current study, during the primary survey, efforts were made to know the views of various teachers and administrators about the parent-teacher association. Most of the teachers and administrators believe that parent-teacher association is slightly influential (40.2%), followed by teachers and administrators who believe that association is somewhat influential (29.1%).
- Proper implementation of the Right to Education Act depends on whether inspectors associated with elementary education visit schools regularly. During the primary survey, an effort was made to know the views of various teachers and administrators related to elementary education, in this regard. Most teachers and administrators believe that inspectors visit schools sometimes (36.8%) and rarely (21.8%). About 6.4% of teachers also felt that inspectors do not visit schools at all.
- The accountability of the inspector of schools also depends on how often in a month or year he visits the schools. Information was obtained from various government and private aided and private unaided teachers and administrators in this regard. Most of the teachers and administrators believed that inspectors of schools were inspected 9-12 months (39.7%) ago, followed by teachers and administrators who felt that inspectors visited schools 6-9 months (31.6%) ago.
- The accountability of elementary education also depends on, whether or not different teachers and administrators maintain regularity and punctuality in schools. In the present study, efforts were made to get their views from various teachers and administrators in this regard. Most of the teachers and administrators believe that they always (35.9%) maintain regularity and punctuality in schools, followed by teachers and administrators who believe that they maintain regularity and punctuality sometimes (26.9%).
- Information was received by various government, private aided and private unaided schools' teachers and administrators

regarding regulations and punctuality of themselves and visits of the inspector of schools. Most of the teachers and administrators felt that they always (15%) maintain regularity and punctuality in schools and the inspector of the school visits the school sometimes. Only 5.6% of teachers and administrators believe and feel that teachers and administrators always maintain regularity and punctuality and inspectors of schools visit schools.

7.2. Observations

7.2.1. Less Computerisation in Government Schools

- During the survey, it was found that all written records are stored in the office of government schools without a computer. Along with this, many such schools were found where a lack of proper records and tracking, etc. was also noticed. In private schools, administrative work is being completed efficiently more by computer than in government schools.

7.2.2. Children and parents discouraged due to poor state of resources

- In government schools, books for children arrive very late and sometimes the books arrive at the school after the completion of the examination.
- Unattractive school environment, unsatisfactory condition of buildings, shortage of teachers, and inadequacy of instructional materials are elements that discourage children and their parents.
- Some government schools were found to interview children and parents before the admission of children. Parents are asked in the interview by education providers about family income, income certificate character certificate, etc.

7.2.3. Parental apathy towards School Management Committee

- During the survey, it was observed that there is a huge lack of information and awareness related to elementary education among parents.
- Teachers as well as parents have a role in the School Management Committee for the proper implementation of the right to education, but problems arise when parents fail to support teachers. During

the survey, many teachers complained that parents' attitude towards coordination with the school is pessimistic.

7.2.4. Teachers' apathy towards their responsibility

- During the survey, it was observed that there is a huge gap between the levels of authority and responsibility of teachers, whereas both rights and responsibilities consist of accountability.
- Many such parents and headmasters were also found who say that the absence of teachers in their school is a big problem.
- Many times, teachers do not try to teach the weaker children separately, they consider it their duty to spend time in school.

7.2.5. Administrative apathy towards teachers and their teaching duties

- During the survey, it was observed that under the Right to Education Act, 25% of poor children are not being admitted to private unaided schools.
- Most of the teacher's time is spent in non-teaching work or school or headmaster's work. Under non-teaching work to teachers, survey work, elections, preparation of school reports from time to time, and other state government duties, etc. All these tasks badly affect the teaching work of the teacher and obstruct the access to proper education.

7.2.6. Administrative apathy in the maintenance of resources in schools

- During the survey, it was observed that the system of feedback in government primary schools is almost non-existent, which is why the accountability of the administrators is not ensured in violation of any provision of the Right to Education Act in government schools.
- It has to be strongly believed that the state of the resources of government schools is not up to the mark, whereas the government is spending a lot of money in this regard. Sometimes, grants are sanctioned for the construction of new buildings, but funds are not provided for the repair and maintenance of the old buildings. The condition of various schools was not found to be correct during the survey. Separate toilets for boys and girls were also not available. Along with the unavailability of proper sanitation, its condition was also not good.

- During the survey, it was observed by the author and told by various teachers about the cleanliness and maintenance of the various resources of the school, such as classrooms, toilets, etc., is not preferred by the administration, due to the absence of children in the school increase is seen.
- During the study, it was observed that there was a huge reduction in the availability of blackboard, due to which the teachers are completing the teaching work without the blackboard. The electricity system was also not proper, and at the same time, the children sat on the jute mats due to the lack of availability of tables and benches. Even in schools where there are tables and benches, their number is much less than the number of children.
- During the survey, some schools were also observed where the headmaster's position was vacant, along with a shortage of teachers in some schools.

7.2.7. Basic Amenities

- Many school buildings, floors walls, etc. were found in poor condition.
- Along with having a separate toilet for boys and girls, it is necessary to pay attention to its cleanliness, which is lacking. Lack of cleanliness and sanitation was also observed, which is one of the main reasons for children to leave school and not attend school.
- The unavailability of clean water and first aid was noticed in many schools. Cleanliness and hygienic conditions were also found to be reduced and some teachers were also told about the poor quality of the mid-day meal, the food is cooked in the open in an unhygienic manner.
- In various government schools, it is commonly seen that students of many classes are studying in the same overcrowded classroom. There can be many reasons and consequences for this. One reason is that there is a huge shortage of teachers along with the classroom, and the result is that children do not get qualitative education properly. Teachers spend all their time disciplining children. Due to the large number of children and the number of children belonging to many classes in the same classroom, it was found to be run outside the classroom, which adversely affects the way of teaching and learning.

- Lack of sports arrangements and lack of sports equipment were seen in almost all schools.

7.2.8. Learning Outcomes

- In the present study, it was observed by the author that in the implementation of the Right to Education Act, there is very little emphasis on learning outputs. Some teachers believe that parents get their children admitted to school, but most of the children never come to school, even if they do not take the exam, they have to pass without examination. This makes the literacy rate increase quantitatively but not qualitatively. If there is a qualitative increase in the resources and education of schools, then the number and attendance of children can also be increased.

7.3. Recommendations

Based on the objectives of the study, and the findings, the following recommendations are made:

7.3.1. For Availability

A. Development of basic infrastructure

- The government should prioritise ensuring both the quantity and quality of available resources. Continuous efforts should be made to maintain this consistency. Additionally, providing separate toilets for boys and girls can help prevent their absence and dropouts.
- Schools should be set up at specific places and not on highways so that various provisions related to the protection of children of the Right to Education Act can be fulfilled.
- Along with the availability of sports equipment and physical education, yoga should also be promoted; time should be fixed for this.
- Classes should not be taken in the open, which disrupts the concentration of children and teachers.
- This study suggested that the availability of benches, electricity, etc. should be facilitated. Whiteboard should be promoted or replaced by blackboard.
- In this study, it is recommended that the top priority should be given to ensuring the availability of clean water and a reliable first aid system.

B. Availability with maintenance of resources

- Maintaining resources in schools is an essential aspect of providing a safe and comfortable learning environment for children, i.e., the availability of resources with 'usability' should be maintained.
- For the proper implementation of the right to education, various educational administrators must take steps regarding the day-to-day evaluation of resources, repair, and maintenance, etc., and with the help of physical inspection in this regard, coordination can be developed with the headmaster who is responsible for the maintenance of resources in the school.
- To maintain school resources, new ideas and research should be encouraged as one of the major reasons for the failure of any government schools is poor resource maintenance.

7.3.2. For Affordability

A. Schooling Setup

- The operation of elementary education is completely carried out by the state government, for the improvement of primary education it is necessary that both the central and state agencies implement the right to education efficiently with cooperation and coordination.
- The most important role in the implementation of the right to education is that of the teachers directly, but in the current system, the teachers are denied the right to take any kind of decisions which have a great impact in their teaching work. For this, it is necessary to make the present system 'participatory' rather than bureaucratic so that decentralisation can be established in the right way and thereby improve the teaching work of teachers as well as increase their accountability.

B. Technology

- There is a lot of potential to improve the implementation of the most cost-effective distribution of resources for primary education through technology.
- Cost-effective methods should be adopted to digitise the distribution of various resources and teaching materials related to elementary school, as well as their availability. Institutional development can envisage improvement in

educational administration by implementing new approaches and adopting cost-effective ideas and best practices.

7.3.3. For Acceptability

A. For Administrators

- Meetings of employees and officers should be held after school hours, classes should not be affected by these meetings.
- During the survey, many teachers said that children do not come to school at all and they have to pass without examination for the next class. For this, special efforts should be taken by the administration to make the mid-day meal qualitative and hygienic; all the cooking materials should be checked continuously, with the help of which the attendance of children in school can be increased to some extent. For this, the concerned officer should also be instructed at different times.
- There should be a provision for strict punishment for violation of any provision of the Right to Education Act so that employees can take their actions seriously.
- There is a need to promote professionalism in government schools like private schools, thereby reducing bossism in government schools. Here, professionalism does not mean making a profit from the children, but it means promoting the management procedure like private schools. By promoting professionalism, cooperation can be increased along with reducing conflict in administration.

B. For Headmasters

- In the city, headmasters should be trained in education to bring quality to the education system in primary schools and self-assessment of schools.
- The headmaster should be taught leadership skills during training so that he can lead teachers and children properly in his school.
- A dashboard report of school achievement related to the quality education system in primary schools of the district should be uploaded online.
- Parent-teacher meetings should always be encouraged in between and efforts should be made to redress the grievances

of the parents. For this, a toll-free number should be mentioned in every school. So that parents can be encouraged to send children to school every day. There is a need to conduct a local awareness campaign to know all the resources related to the school and the right to education.

C. For Teachers

- Vacant posts of teachers should be filled as soon as possible. In addition, the minimum availability of teachers per classroom should be maintained.
- For teacher training, there is a need to decentralise the development of training centres. Periodically various block resource centres should be allowed to build these with the help of teachers.
- Teachers should not be given the responsibility to complete tasks such as survey-related work, election duties, surveys for below poverty line (BPL) persons, preparation for electoral rolls, etc. other than teaching. Due to this, the teaching time and efficiency of teachers are greatly affected.
- Dissatisfaction with the present promotion system was also observed among the teachers, for whom the system of promotion should be reviewed. In this regard, it is necessary to keep their qualifications in mind, and everyone should also be given equal opportunity for promotion.

7.3.4. For Adaptability

A. For Children

- In the study, it is recommended that students of different classes should be educated in separate classrooms only, so that efficient teaching work can be done by teachers.

B. For Parents

- To strengthen the school management committee in primary schools, parents should also be trained now, and they should be made aware of the importance of education so that they can send their children to school every day.
- The administration should train the parents of the children with the help of different Non-Governmental Organisations (NGOs) from time to time so that the parents can take an interest in the education of the children; and ensure their

participation in the programmes organised in the schools from time to time.

- The information about the meetings being held from time to time by the School Management Committee should be made online so that the accountability of the administration in this regard can be ensured.
- Community-based information obtained from micro-planning and surveys should be correlated with school-level data.

C. Parental awareness for effective implementation of the right to education

- Education of children can be improved through awareness of parents towards the School Management Committee.
- Seminars should be organised to make parents aware of education.
- Children and their parents should be informed about the government facilities in schools through pamphlets, mobile phones, internet, etc.

7.3.5. For Accountability

A. To meet the objectives of any organisation, accountability can be increased by keeping in mind the following 4P's

1. **People:** They are the only people who perform, not technology and strategy, etc. When accountability is promoted, people have to feel safe and valued as well as ensure their care.
2. **Purpose:** A 'supportive work environment' can be developed through accountability to inculcate a shared sense of purpose among employees. The main objective of accountability is to advance the vision of the organisation as well as empower employees to perform, focus on achieving the goals, and also to prepare the progress and results.
3. **Performance:** Accountability for performance ensures that all people associated with the organisation are playing their important role. Focusing on performance increases the morale of the employees and also prevents the deterioration in the ethics and integrity of the employees so that they are not in a position to compromise their values.

4. **Progression:** The progress of the organisation can be increased to a higher level by employees by consistently achieving performance goals through accountability.

B. Keeping in mind the 4Ps mentioned above, the following recommendations related to accountability can be implemented

1. Authority and responsibility should be seen as sub-indicators of Accountability
   - As mentioned in the observations, there was a huge gap in the level of authority and responsibility among teachers, headmasters, and administrators. For this, along with responsibility, proper authority should also be given to the teachers and headmasters so that they can work with high morale.
2. Computerisation of Educational Administration
   - To increase the accountability of the administration through e-governance, the written work and records of all schools must be completed through computerisation.
   - With the computerisation of administrative work in schools, teachers can get more time in teaching work and can complete syllabi in a time-bound manner.
   - Whatever the delay in reaching the teaching materials in schools, this deficiency can be overcome by coordinating with the educational administration through networking and quick decision-making.
   - Through computerisation, the implementation of the right to education can be made more cost-effective, transparent, and efficient.
   - Simultaneously, with the help of computerisation for organisational change, the work culture of government schools can be made smarter.
   - By removing various hurdles in education through computerisation, with eradicating the malfunction at school, the right to education of children can be protected along with the satisfaction of their parents.
   - Apart from this, every school should be motivated to give complete information to the community, even information about the grant. For this, every school should have a notice

board. This can increase the accountability of headmaster and other administrators at the school level.

3. Accountability through proper Monitoring system and Inspections
   - Accountability can be increased at various levels by properly implementing the monitoring system to assess the effectiveness of implementing the right to education. There is a need to improve the block-specific monitoring system which can involve the local community.
   - Feedback system should be arranged at the block and school level so that attempts can be made to resolve the problems of the parents.
   - An effective monitoring function can be implemented only by finding relevant data, analyzing it, and turning it into evidence. Good decisions at the school level require good data for which confidential inquiries are also essential.
   - There should be a code of conduct for all teachers and administrators associated with primary education, through which to monitor the education providers as well as to prevent corruption, irregularity of duty, violation of provisions negligence, etc.
4. Toll-free for Easy Communication
   - The toll-free numbers for parents should be mentioned on the walls or notice boards of every school, with the help of which they can solve their problems as well as get the necessary information related to the school.
   - Complaint windows should be installed at the Post Office, Aadhaar centre, or State Bank of India (SBI) along with toll-free numbers.
5. Amenability for Grievance Redressal System
   - To properly implement the right to education, children, parents, and voluntary organisations must be provided with a judicial or quasi-judicial forum where they can share their problems and protect their rights. For this, an independent and impartial judicial or quasi-judicial forum should be established at the block level and an ombudsperson should be appointed to increase the amenability in administration for equitable and justiciable right to education without undue

delay. This could be an example of a decentralised tribunal for primary education.

6. Admissibility of Complaints

- Providing adaptability to the complaints of children and parents on violation of the right to education and admissibility of complaints is also very important for educational administration.

7.4. Conclusion

The implementation of primary education universally for both the central and state governments has been the biggest challenge in India since independence. There is no doubt that primary school is the foundation of higher education. It is a place where the all-round development of the child takes place. The role of administrators along with parents and teachers is very important to achieve the objectives of qualitative primary education; nothing can be finalised without the cooperation of one of these people. Therefore, everyone should feel that it protects their interests and that primary school is their own, it is their responsibility to run it in the best way as they can give ideas for monitoring and evaluation of primary education to policymakers and those who implement it, which ultimately promotes social efficiency to achieve the ultimate goal of the nation. All primary schools in Varanasi in particular can adopt these methods to provide quality education for children. The District Education Officer must direct all inspectors concerned with primary education to go to urban and semi-urban areas as well as rural areas and identify schools that are running without any basic facilities and resources. When we start getting such a list of schools, the concerned authorities can focus on these problems. Coordination can be done with school authorities with technical help so that solutions to various problems as well as school resources and other needs can be met immediately.

Bibliography

Bibliography

Aayog, N. I. T. I. (2019). School Education Quality Index.

Act, N. C. L. B. (2002). *No Child Left Behind Act of 2001.* Publ. L, 107-110.

Act, R. T. E. (2009). *The right of children to free and compulsory education act.* Published in Part II, Section, 1.

Act, R. T. E. (2009). *The right of children to free and compulsory education act 2009.* The Gazette of India.

Addonizio, M., & Kearney, C. P. (2012). *Education reform and the limits of policy: Lessons from Michigan.* WE Upjohn Institute.

Aggarwal, J. C. (1992). *Education policy in India: 1992 and review 2000 and 2005.* Shipra Publications.

Aggarwal, J. C. (2007). *Development of the education system in India.* Shipra.

Altekar, A. S. (2009). *Education in ancient India.* Gyan Publishing House.

ASER (Annual Status of Education Report), 2014.

ASER (Annual Status of Education Report), 2015.

ASER. (2013). *District Performance Tables: Uttar Pradesh.*

ASER. (2014). *District Performance Tables: Uttar Pradesh.*

ASER. (2014). Uttar Pradesh. *Analysis Based on Data From Households.* 69 Out of 69 Districts.

Assembly, U. G. (2000). *United Nations Millennium Declaration.* Resolution adopted by the General Assembly 55/2, 8 September.

Bakshi, P. M. (2013). *Concurrent powers of legislation under List III of the Constitution.* Ministry of Law and Justice. Accessed on June 9, 2014.

Barakat, B. (2016). *Improving adult literacy without improving the literacy of adults?* A cross-national cohort analysis. World Development, 87, 242-257.

Basu, R. (1994). *Public administration: Concepts and theories.* Sterling Publishers Pvt. Ltd.

Bhagia, N., Briggs, D., & Bhagia, S. (1990). *Educational administration in India and other developing countries: Challenges, tasks and training.* Commonwealth Publishers.

Bhattacharya, S. (1955, January). *The Men Who Ruled India, 1899—1901 (A sketch by Lord Curzon): In Proceedings of the Indian History Congress* (Vol. 18, pp. 209-216). Indian History Congress.

Brief, C. I. P. (2010). Pre-Primary Education in India.

Brief, C. I. P. (2011). Effective School Management Committees.

Brief, C. I. P. (2011). Teachers and Teaching in India.

Bryman, A. (2012). *Social research methods.* OUP Oxford.

Buckland, P. (2000). *Making quality basic education affordable: what have we learned*? New York: UNICEF Cameron.

Center, A. S. E. R. (2018). *Annual Status of Education Report.* New Delhi: ASER Center.

Chavan, M. (August 2012). *Elementary education: Access to what?* Yojana, 56, 53-55.

Cheminais, R. (2014). *Special educational needs for qualified and trainee teachers: A practical guide to the new changes.* Routledge.

Child labour and exploitation. (2011). Unicef India. Retrieved from https://www.unicef.org/india/what-we-do/child-labour-exploitation.

Cohen, L., Manion, L., & Morrison, K. (2013). *Research methods in education.* Routledge.

Craissati, D. (2007). *A human rights-based approach to education for all: a framework for the realisation of children's right to education and rights within education.* New York: United Nations Children's Fund.

Creswell, J. W. (1998). *Qualitative research and research design: Choosing among five traditions.* London: Thousand Oaks, CA: Sage Publications.

Delphine Dorsi. (2014, December 10). *The Right to Education: a Daily Challenge.* https://www.right-to-education.org/blog/right-education-daily-challenge.

Denhardt, R. B., & Grubbs, J. W. (2003). *Public administration: An action orientation (p. 36).* United States: Thomson and Wadsworth.

Dossing, H. (2011). *Mapping transparency, accountability, and integrity in primary education in South Africa.* Transparency International.

Dreze, J., & Kingdon, G. G. (1999). *School Participation in Rural India: The Development Economics Discussion Paper Series, No. 18.* London: London School of Economics.

Dreze, J., & Sen, A. (1999). *India: Economic development and social opportunity.* OUP Catalogue.

Drucker, P. F. (2004). *What makes an effective executive?* Harvard Business Review, 82(6).

Edmondson, R. (2012, July 2). *3 Keys to Effective Accountability.* https://ronedmondson.com/2012/07/3-keys-to-effective-accountability.html.

Elementary Education in India, (2016). NUEPA, 2016. Retrieved from http://dise.in/Downloads/Elementary-STRC-2015-16/Elementary-State_Report_ Cards_2015-16.pdf

Gaind, D. N., & Sharma, R. P. (1966). *Education and Secondary School Administration.* Ram Prasad.

Gary, T. (2011). *How to do your case study: A guide for students and researchers.* Thousand Oaks, CA: Sage Publications.

Gladden, E. N. (2019). *A History of Public Administration: Volume I: From the Earliest Times to the Eleventh Century.* Routledge.

Glueck, W. F. (1974). *Personnel: A diagnostic approach.* Business Publications.

Government of India (1992). *National policy on education 1986.* Programme of action, 1992.

Govinda, R., & Bandyopadhyay, M. (2008). *Access to elementary education in India.* Consortium for Research on Educational Access, Transitions and Equity (CREATE).

Govinda, R., & Bandyopadhyay, M. *Achieving Universal Elementary Education in India: Expanding Access with Equity.* NUEPA, New Delhi, 1-37.

Haggis, S. M. (1991). *Education for All: Purpose and Context.* World Conference on Education for All (Jomtien, Thailand, March 5-9, 1990). Monograph I. Roundtable Themes I. Unesco Press, 7, place de Fontenoy, 75700 Paris, France.

Harsch, E. (2000). *Dakar summit urges renewed global drive to achieve basic education for all.* Africa Recovery, 14(2), 14-18.

Hazra, A. (May 2011). *The Challenge of Educating Rural India.* Kurukshetra, 59(7), 3-5.

Helfer, L. R., & Austin, G. W. (2011). *Human rights and intellectual property: Mapping the global interface.* Cambridge University Press.

History of child rights, (2020). Unicef, for every child, 2020. Retrieved from https://www.unicef.org/child-rights-convention/history-child-rights

Hughes, O. E. (2012). *Public management and administration: An introduction.* Macmillan International Higher Education.

India, A. S. E. R. (2014). *Annual status of education report (rural) 2013.* ASER Centre, New Delhi.

India, A. S. E. R. (2017). *Annual status of education report (rural) 2013.* ASER Centre, New Delhi.

International Covenant on Civil and Political Rights, (2020). United Nations Human Rights, 2020. Retrieved from https://www.ohchr.org/en/professionalinterest/ pages/ccpr.aspx

Jahoda, M., & Barnitz, E. (1955). *The nature of evaluation.* International Social Science Bulletin, 7(3), 1-13.

Jain, S. C. (2002). *The Constitution (Eighty-Sixth Amendment) Act.* New Delhi: Government of India.

Jayapalan, N. (2005). *History of education in India.* Atlantic Publishers & Distributors.

Jha, D., & Tripathi, V. (2014). *Quality of life in slums of Varanasi city: a comparative study.* Transactions, 36(2).

Jha, J., Ghatak, N., Chandrashekaran, S., Mahendiran, S., Minni, P., Bakshi, S., & Thyagrajan, R. (2013). *Challenges in Implementing the Right to Education: The Karnataka Case.* Centre for Budget and Policy Studies Working Paper.

Jha, P., & Parvati, P. (2010). *Right to Education Act 2009: critical gaps and challenges.* Economic and Political Weekly, 20-23.

Joyita, 2013. The Mid-Day Meal Scheme. (2017, July 7). Retrieved from https://www.prsindia.org/theprsblog/mid-day-meal-scheme

Kainth, G. S. (2006). *A mission approach to Sarva Shiksha Abhiyan.* Economic and Political Weekly, 3288-3291.

Kaul, V., & Sankar, D. (2009). *Early childhood care and education in India.* Education for All Mid-Decade Assessment. New Delhi, India, National University of Educational Planning and Administration (NUEPA).

Klees, S. J., & Thapliyal, N. (2007). *The right to education: The work of Katarina Tomasevski.* Comparative Education Review, 51(4), 497-510.

Kothari, C. R. (2004). *Research methodology: Methods and techniques.* New Age International.

Kothari, D. S. (1970). *Education, science, and national development.* Asia Publishing House.

Kumar, A. (1991). *Current trends in Indian education.* APH Publishing.

Latitude and Longitude of Uttar Pradesh, (2011). Map of India, 2011. Retrieved from https://www.mapsofindia.com/lat_long/uttarpradesh/

Leedy, P. D., & Ormrod, J. E. (2013). *Practical research: Planning and design*. Boston, MA: Merrill.

Maheshwari, V. K. (2012). *Evolution of Educational System in India*. Retrieved from http://www.vkmaheshwari.com/WP/?p=528

Malan, T. (1987). *Educational planning as a social process* (No. 33-37). Unipub.

Mathur, M. V. (1983). *Towards Improved Educational Planning and Administration*. Joy Madhathi Kunnel for Dialogue, New Delhi.

Mehrotra, S. K. (Ed.). (2005). *Universalizing elementary education in India: Uncaging the 'tiger' economy*. Oxford University Press, USA.

Mehrotra, S., & Panchamukhi, P. R. (2006). *Private provision of elementary education in India: Findings of a survey in eight states*. Compare, 36(4), 421-442.

Mishra, R. C. (2007). *History of education administration*. APH Pub.

Mondal, A. (2017). *Free and Compulsory Primary Education in India under the British Raj: A Tale of an Unfulfilled Dream*. SAGE Open, 7(3), 2158244017727037.

Mwinjuma, J. S. (2015). *A Review of Characteristics and Experiences of Decentralisation of Education*. International Journal of Education and Literacy Studies, 3(1), 34-41.

Naik, J. P. (1965). *Educational planning in India*. Allied Publishers.

Nigro, L. G., Nigro, F. A., & Kellough, J. E. (2012). *The new public personnel administration*. Cengage Learning.

Pal, Y. (August 2012). *An optimistic future for Indian Education*. Yojana, 56, 5-7.

Pandya, D. R. N. (2014). *Indian education system: a historical journey*. Education, 3(3).

Pierce, C. (2012). *Education in the age of bio capitalism: Optimizing educational life for a flat world*. Springer.

Pritchett, L., & Pande, V. (2006). *Making Primary Education Work for India's Rural Poor: A Proposal for Effective Decentralisation*. New Delhi: World Bank.

Puar, S. S. (2012). *Right to Education Act: A critical analysis*. International Journal of Educational and Psychological Research (IJEPR), 1(2), 27-30.

Purvis, B., Mao, Y., & Robinson, D. (2019). *Three pillars of sustainability: in search of conceptual origins*. Sustainability science, 14(3), 681-695.

Raffel, J. A. (2007). *Why has public administration ignored public education, and does it matter?* Public Administration Review, 67(1), 135-151.

Raghavan, J. V. (1986). *Implementation of the New Education Policy-1986*. Indian Journal of Public Administration, 32(3), 521-534.

Report of Workshop on Educational Development Index (EDI) (2014, July 30). NUEPA, 2014. Retrieved from http://www.dise.in/Downloads/EDI%20workshop%20report.pdf

Right to Education (2014). Section 18. No school is to be established without obtaining a certificate of recognition. Retrieved from http://righttoeducation.in/forums/suggest-rte-amendments/section-18-no-school-to-be-established-without-obtaining-certificate-of-recognition

Right to Education (2014). Section 6. Duty of appropriate Government and local authority to establish a school. Retrieved from http://righttoeducation.in/forums/suggest-rte-amendments/ section-6-duty-of-appropriate-government-and-local-authority-to-establish-school#forum-topic-top

Right to Education, (2014). Section 12. Extent of school's responsibility for free and compulsory education. Retrieved from http://righttoeducation.in/forums/suggest-rte-amendments/section-12-extent-of-schools-responsibility-for-free-and-compulsory-education

Right to Education, (2014). Section 13. No capitation fee or screening procedure for admission. Retrieved from http://righttoeducation.in/forums/suggest-rte-amendments/section-13-no-capitation-fee-and-screening-procedure-for-admission

Right to Education, (2014). Section 21. School Management Committee. Retrieved from http:// righttoeducation.in/forums/suggest-rte-amendments/section-21-school-management-committee

Right to Education, (2014). Section 23. Qualifications for appointment and terms and conditions of service of teachers. Retrieved from http://righttoeducation.in/forums/suggest-rte-amendments/

Right to Education, (2014). Section 24. Duties of teachers and redressal of grievances. Retrieved from http://righttoeducation.in/forums/suggest-rte-amendments/section-24-duties-of-teachers-and-redressal-of-grievances

Right to Education, (2014). Section 4. Special provisions for children not admitted to, or who have not completed elementary education. Retrieved from http://righttoeducation.in/forums/ suggest-rte-amendments/section-4-special-provisions-for-children-not-admitted-to-or-who-have-not-completed-elementary-education

Right to Education, (2014). Section 7. Sharing of financial and other responsibilities. Retrieved from http://righttoeducation.in/forums/suggest-rte-amendments/section-7-sharing-of-financial-and-other-responsibilities

Ring, T., & Salkin, R. M. (1996). *International dictionary of historic places.* Fitzroy Dearborn Publishers.

Sahni, U. (2015). *Primary education in India: Progress and challenges.* The second Modi-Obama summit: Building the India-US partnership, 35-38.

Santiago, P., McGregor, I., Nusche, D., Ravela, P., & Toledo, D. (2012). *OECD Reviews of Evaluation and Assessment in Education: Mexico.* OECD Publishing.

Sapru, R. K. (2008). *Administrative theories and management thought.* PHI Learning Pvt. Ltd.

Sarangapani, P. M., Mehendale, A., Mukhopadhyay, R., & Namala, A. (2014). *Inclusion of marginalised children in private unaided schools.* The RTE Act, 2009.

Sarkar, S. (1989). *Modern India 1885–1947.* Springer.

Sarva Siksha Abhiyan (SSA), *Manual for District- Level Functionaries. (2017).* MHRD, 1–199. Retrieved from https://darpg.gov.in/sites/default/files/Sarva%20Siksha%20 Abhiyan.pdf

Satyarthi, K. (November 2012). *Preparing for the new child labour law.* Yojana, 56, 19-21.

School Education in India, (2016). NUEPA, 2016. Retrieved from http://www.dise.in/Downloads/Publications/Documents/U-DISE-SchoolEducationInIndia-2015-16.pdf

Schools in Arunachal Pradesh, (2020). In Schools, 2020. Retrieved from https://www.inschools.in/state/Arunachal-Pradesh.html/section-23-qualifications-for- appointment-and-terms-and-conditions-of-service-of-teachers

Setting standards for schools. (2016, July 13). The Hindu, 2016. Retrieved from https://www.thehindu.com/opinion/op-ed/setting-standards-for-schools/article7735243.ece

Sharma, Y. K. (2001). *History and problems of education* (Vol. 1). Kanishka Publishers.

Simon, H. A. (2013). *Administrative behavior.* Simon and Schuster.

Sinclair, P. (2014). *Basics in Education.* Text Book for B. Ed Course.

Singh, J. (2014). *Article 21A (Right to education): Critical analysis.* Asian Journal of Multidimensional Research (AJMR), 3(3), 45-50.

Slesinger, D., & Stephenson, M. (1930). *The Encyclopaedia of Social Sciences.* Vol. IX. MacMillan.

Social Demography, (2011). Retrieved from http://up.gov.in/Social-Demography.pdf

Source, D. Government of India (website: http://mhrd.gov.in/statist). *Educational Statistics at a Glance (2018).* Published By: Government of India, Ministry of Human Resource Development, New Delhi.

Spreen, C. A., & Vally, S. (2010). *Prospects and pitfalls: A review of post-apartheid education policy research and analysis in South Africa.* Comparative Education, 46(4), 429-448.

Takwale, R., Sawant, V., & Deshmukh, M. N. (2010). *NaiTalim and Gandhian Approaches to Development.* North-South Dialogues.

The Constitution (Eighty-Sixth Amendment) Act, (2002). National Portal of India, 2012. Retrieved from https://www.india.gov.in/my-government/constitution-india/amendments/constitution-india-eighty-sixth-amendment-act-2002

The Gazette of India, (2009). The Right of Children to Free and Compulsory Education Act, (2009). Retrieved from https://mhrd.gov.in/sites/upload_files/mhrd/files/upload_document/rte.pdf

The Gazette of India, (2019). The Right of Children to Free and Compulsory Education (Amendment) Act, 2019. Retrieved from https://mhrd.gov.in/sites/upload_files/mhrd/files/ upload_document/rte_2019.pdf

The Hindu, (2014, November 26). Retrieved from http://en.kiosko.net/in/2014-11-26/np/hindu. html. Pg.11

The Right of Children to Free and Compulsory Education Act, (2009). Clarification on Provisions. Retrieved from https://mhrd.gov.in/sites/upload_files/mhrd/files/ upload_document/RTE_Section_ wise_rationale_rev_0.pdf

The Right of Children to Free and Compulsory Education Act, 2009. Clarification on Provisions. Retrieved from https://mhrd.gov.in/sites/upload_files/mhrd/files/ upload_document/RTE_Section_

The Sargent Report: Objects, Criticism and Defects: Education. (2016, August 30). Yourarticlelibrary, 2019. Retrieved from http://www.yourarticlelibrary.com/ education/the-Sargent-report-objects-criticism-and-defects-education/89644

Thirumalai, M. S. (2003). *Lord Macaulay: The man who started it all, and his Minute.* Language in India, 3(4).

Tilak, J. B. (1988). *Vocational education in South Asia: Problems and prospects.* International Review of Education, 244-257.

Tilak, J. B. (1996*). How free is 'free' primary education in India?* Economic and Political Weekly, 355-366.

Tomasevski, K. (2001). *Human rights obligations: making education available, accessible, acceptable, and adaptable.* Raoul Wallenberg Institute of Human Rights and Humanitarian Law.

Tomaševski, Katarina. (2003). *Education denied: costs and remedies.* New York: Zed Books.

UK. (2013). *Primary assessment and accountability under the new national curriculum.* Department of Education, UK.

UNICEF, I., & UNICEF, (2011). *The situation of children in India: a profile.* New Delhi: UNICEF.

UNICEF. (2007). *A human rights-based approach to education for all: A framework for the realisation of children's right to education and rights within education.* United Nations Publications.

Varanasi District Population Census, (2011-2020). Uttar Pradesh literacy, sex ratio and density, 2011. Retrieved from https://www.census2011.co.in/census/ district/568-varanasi.html

Varghese, N. V. (1996). *Decentralisation of educational planning in India: The case of the district primary education programme.* International Journal of Educational Development, 16(4), 355-365.

Vasavi, A. R. (2006). *Caste indignities and subjected personhoods.* Economic and Political Weekly, 3766-3771.

Waldo, D. (2006). *The administrative state: A study of the political theory of American public administration.* Transaction Publishers.

Wardha Scheme of Basic Education (1937). NeoStencil, 2019. Retrieved from https://neostencil.com/upsc-modern-history-wardha-scheme-basic-education-1937

Werner, J. (2009). *Public administration in the education sector: boon or bane for Western Europe?* International Public Management Review, 10(2), 1-22.

Wilcox, B. (2000). *Making school inspection visits more effective: The English experience.* UNESCO, International Institute for Educational Planning.

Williams, C. (2007). *Research methods.* Journal of Business & Economics Research (JBER), 5(3).

Wilson, W. (1955). *The study of public administration* (Vol. 744, No. 24). Public Affairs Press. wise_rationale_rev_0.pdf

Yamane, T. (1967). *Problems to accompany "Statistics, an introductory analysis".* Harper & Row.

Appendices

Appendices

APPENDIX - I

INTERVIEW SCHEDULE FOR PARENTS

Introduction

This Interview Schedule is a part of Ph.D. thesis work in the Department of Political Science, Banaras Hindu University (BHU), Varanasi.

Research Scholar	:	Ritesh Kumar Agarwal
Supervisor	:	Dr. Abhinav Sharma, Associate Professor, BHU, Varanasi
Topic of Research	:	*"The Role of Administration in Right to Education (RTE): A Case Study of Varanasi, U.P."*

Note: - *The information asked in this schedule is exclusively for research purpose and will be kept strictly confidential.*

Part – I: General Information

1.	Name	Shri/Smt____________________	
2.	Occupation	(a) Government Job	( )
		(b) Private Job	( )
		(c) Business	( )
		(d) Agriculture	( )
		(e) Others	( )
3.	Income	(a) 0-50 thousand/annum	( )
		(b) 50 thousand- 1 lakh/annum	( )
		(c) 1-2 lakhs/annum	( )
		(d) 2-5 lakhs/annum	( )
		(e) 5 lakhs and above/annum	( )
4.	Address	____________________	
		____________________	
		____________________	
5.	Contact No. (If any)	____________________	

6. Name and address of your child's School ______________________________

____

____

7. Type of School
   (a) Government ( )
   (b) Private aided ( )
   (c) Private unaided ( )

8. Organisation of School
   (a) Boys ( )
   (b) Girls ( )
   (c) Co-ed ( )

9. Location of the School
   (a) Urban ( )
   (b) Semi - urban ( )

Part - II: Examine the Main Constituents of Access to Primary Education

1. What do you think about the opportunities your child has to learn about different subjects?
   (a) Poor ( )
   (b) Fair ( )
   (c) Good ( )
   (d) Very good ( )
   (e) Excellent ( )

2. Is your child is learning what he or she needs to know?
   (a) Strongly disagree ( )
   (b) Disagree ( )
   (c) Neither agree or disagree ( )
   (d) Agree ( )
   (e) Strongly agree ( )

3. Is your child clearly understands what he or she is expected to learn at school?
   (a) Never ( )
   (b) Rarely ( )
   (c) Sometimes ( )
   (d) Often ( )
   (e) Always ( )

4. Is your child finds school work interesting?
   (a) Never ( )
   (b) Almost never ( )
   (c) Occasionally/sometimes ( )

(d) Almost every time ( )

(e) Every time ( )

5. Is your child finds school work challenging?

(a) Never ( )

(b) Almost never ( )

(c) Occasionally/sometimes ( )

(d) Almost every time ( )

(e) Every time ( )

Part – III: To Develop Suitable Indicators of 4A (Availability, Affordability, Acceptability and Adaptability)

1. Are you satisfied with the quality of education your child is receiving at school?

(a) Not at all satisfied ( )

(b) Slightly satisfied ( )

(c) Moderately satisfied ( )

(d) Very satisfied ( )

(e) Extremely satisfied ( )

2. What do you think about the opportunities your child has to participate in physical education at school?

(a) Not at all influential ( )

(b) Slightly influential ( )

(c) Somewhat influential ( )

(d) Very influential ( )

(e) Extremely influential ( )

3. Are you satisfied with the special support your child has received at school?

(a) Not at all satisfied ( )

(b) Slightly satisfied ( )

(c) Moderately satisfied ( )

(d) Very satisfied ( )

(e) Extremely satisfied ( )

4. Is your child's school environment supports learning?

(a) Not at all familiar ( )

(b) Slightly familiar ( )

(c) Somewhat familiar ( )

(d) Moderately family ( )

(e) Extremely familiar ( )

5. Which subject do you find to be the most difficult for your child?
   (a) Hindi/Sanskrit ( )
   (b) English ( )
   (c) Maths ( )
   (d) Science ( )
   (e) Social Science ( )

Part – IV: To Identify the Possibilities of an Accountable Educational Administration

1. Are you satisfied with the opportunity to be involved in decisions at your child's school?
   (a) Not at all satisfied ( )
   (b) Slightly satisfied ( )
   (c) Moderately satisfied ( )
   (d) Very satisfied ( )
   (e) Extremely satisfied ( )
2. Are you satisfied with your input into decisions at your child's school is considered?
   (a) Much worse ( )
   (b) Somewhat worse ( )
   (c) About the same ( )
   (d) Somewhat better ( )
   (e) Much better ( )
3. Is your child safe at school?
   (a) Strongly disagree ( )
   (b) Disagree ( )
   (c) Neither agree or disagree ( )
   (d) Agree ( )
   (e) Strongly agree ( )
4. Is teachers care about your child?
   (a) Not at all concerned ( )
   (b) Slightly concerned ( )
   (c) Somewhat concerned ( )
   (d) Moderately concerned ( )
   (e) Extremely concerned ( )
5. Is your child is treated fairly by teachers at school?
   (a) Never use ( )

(b) Almost never ( )

(c) Occasionally/sometimes ( )

(d) Almost every time ( )

(e) Frequently use ( )

6. Is your child's school facilities are clean and well-maintained?

(a) Very undesirable ( )

(b) Undesirable ( )

(c) Neutral ( )

(d) Desirable ( )

(e) Very desirable ( )

7. Is teacher(s)/school tells to you about your child's academic progress, challenges and successes?

(a) Never ( )

(b) Rarely ( )

(c) Occasionally ( )

(d) A moderate amount ( )

(e) A great deal ( )

8. Is your child's school is sensitive to issues regarding race, gender, sexual orientation and disabilities?

(a) Not a priority ( )

(b) Low priority ( )

(c) Medium priority ( )

(d) High priority ( )

(e) Essential ( )

9. What do you think about the behaviour of the teachers and administrators of your child's school?

(a) Inappropriate ( )

(b) Slightly inappropriate ( )

(c) Neutral ( )

(d) Slightly appropriate ( )

(e) Appropriate ( )

10. Does your child's school administration communicate with you?

(a) Never ( )

(b) Rarely ( )

(c) Sometimes ( )

(d) Often ( )

(e) Always ( )

11. What do you think about your child's school curriculum?

(a) Not at all influential ( )

(b) Slightly influential ( )

(c) Somewhat influential ( )

(d) Very influential ( )

(e) Extremely influential ( )

12. What do you think about the difficulty of language for learning in your child's school?

(a) Very difficult ( )

(b) Difficult ( )

(c) Neutral ( )

(d) Easy ( )

(e) Very easy ( )

13. Is there any health facility in your child's school?

(a) Very undesirable ( )

(b) Undesirable ( )

(c) Neutral ( )

(d) Desirable ( )

(e) Very desirable ( )

14. What do you think about the administrative problems of your child's school?

____

____

15. Academic problems ______________________________

____

16. Financial problems ______________________________

____

17. Any other problems (please specify)______________________

____

18. What is your opinion about the standard of primary education? (Please state)

____

____

____

APPENDIX – II

INTERVIEW SCHEDULE FOR TEACHERS AND ADMINISTRATORS

Introduction:	:	This Interview Schedule is a part of Ph.D. thesis work in the Department of Political Science, Banaras Hindu University, Varanasi.
Research Scholar	:	Ritesh Kumar Agarwal
Supervisor	:	Dr. Abhinav Sharma, Associate Professor, B.H.U. Varanasi
Topic of Research	:	*"The Role of Administration in Right to Education (RTE): A Case Study of Varanasi, U.P."*

Note: *- The information asked in this schedule is exclusively for research purpose and will be kept strictly confidential.*

Part –I: General Information

1.	Name	Shri/Smt____________________________	
2.	Designation	(a) Teacher	( )
		(b) Administrator	( )
3.	Qualification	(a) High School	( )
		(b) Intermediate	( )
		(c) Graduation	( )
		(d) Post Graduation and above	( )

4. Teaching experience (Please specify the year)__________________________

5. Name and address of the School

____

____

6. Year of Establishment ____

7. Year of recognition by the Government______________________________

8.	Type of School	(a) Government	( )
		(b) Private aided	( )
		(c) Private unaided	( )
9.	Organisation of School	(a) Boys	( )
		(b) Girls	( )
		(c) Co-ed	( )
10.	Location of the School	(a) Urban	( )
		(b) Semi - urban	( )
11.	Classes from	(a) UKG to Class VIII	( )
		(b) UKG to Class X	( )
		(c) UKG to Class XII	( )

Part – II: Examine the Main Constituents of Access to Primary Education

Availability: *Availability is that education is free and government funded and that there is adequate infrastructure and trained teachers able to support education delivery.

Affordability: *Affordability is that the system is non-discriminatory and accessible to all, and that positive steps are taken to include the most marginalised.

1. Is the School Building structurally safe?
   (a) Much worse ( )
   (b) Somewhat worse ( )
   (c) About the same ( )
   (d) Somewhat better ( )
   (e) Much better ( )
2. Does each classroom have enough desks and benches for students?
   (a) Strongly disagree ( )
   (b) Disagree ( )
   (c) Neither agree or disagree ( )
   (d) Agree ( )
   (e) Strongly agree ( )
3. Are the classrooms spacious enough?
   (a) Very undesirable ( )
   (b) Undesirable ( )
   (c) Neutral ( )
   (d) Desirable ( )
   (e) Very desirable ( )
4. Does the school provide any hostel or boarding for students?
   (a) Strongly disagree ( )
   (b) Disagree ( )
   (c) Neither agree or disagree ( )
   (d) Agree ( )
   (e) Strongly agree ( )
5. Is education accessible to all, without discrimination on any grounds for example race, colour, ethnicity, and sex, language, and religion, social and economic status?
   (a) Strongly disagree ( )
   (b) Disagree ( )
   (c) Neither agree or disagree ( )

(d) Agree ( )

(e) Strongly agree ( )

6. Is education within safe physical reach?

(a) Strongly disagree ( )

(b) Disagree ( )

(c) Neither agree or disagree ( )

(d) Agree ( )

(e) Strongly agree ( )

7. Are there appropriate transport facilities?

(a) Inappropriate ( )

(b) Slightly inappropriate ( )

(c) Neutral ( )

(d) Slightly appropriate ( )

(e) Appropriate ( )

8. Are there sufficient teachers?

(a) Insufficient ( )

(b) Somewhat insufficient ( )

(c) Neither insufficient nor sufficient ( )

(d) Somewhat sufficient ( )

(e) Sufficient ( )

9. Who recruits the teacher in your school? (Please tick)

(a) Headmaster/Headmistress ( )

(b) Managing Committee ( )

(c) District Education Officer ( )

(d) State Director of Elementary Education ( )

(e) Any other ( )

10. Does the school have adequate playgrounds and open spaces for recreation?

(a) Insufficient ( )

(b) Somewhat insufficient ( )

(c) Neither insufficient nor sufficient ( )

(d) Somewhat sufficient ( )

(e) Sufficient ( )

11. Do you have facilities for medical check-up for your students?

(a) Inappropriate ( )

(b) Slightly inappropriate ( )

(c) Neutral ( )

(d) Slightly appropriate ( )

(e) Appropriate ( )

Part – III: To develop suitable indicators of 4A (Availability, Affordability, Acceptability and Adaptability)

Acceptability: *Acceptability is that the content of education is relevant, non-discriminatory, culturally appropriate, and of quality; that the school itself is safe and teachers are professional.

Adaptability: *Adaptability is that education can evolve with the changing needs of society and contribute to challenging inequalities, such as gender discrimination, and that it can be adapted locally to suit specific contexts.

1. Does the school have a good communication network?

   (a) Not at all influential ( )

   (b) Slightly influential ( )

   (c) Somewhat influential ( )

   (d) Very influential ( )

   (e) Extremely influential ( )

2. Is there any scope for future extension and improvement of the school?

   (a) Not probable ( )

   (b) Somewhat improbable ( )

   (c) Neutral ( )

   (d) Somewhat probable ( )

   (e) Very probable ( )

3. Which facility is extremely not available in your school?

   (a) Office Room ( )

   (b) Urinal and Lavatories ( )

   (c) Drinking water ( )

   (d) Library ( )

   (e) Any Other ( )

4. Are teachers well trained?

   (a) Strongly disagree ( )

   (b) Disagree ( )

   (c) Neither agree or disagree ( )

   (d) Agree ( )

   (e) Strongly agree ( )

5. Do they receive domestically competitive salaries?
   - (a) Never ( )
   - (b) Rarely ( )
   - (c) Sometimes ( )
   - (d) Often ( )
   - (e) Always ( )

6. Do they have appropriate working conditions, teaching material, and the right to organise?
   - (a) Not at all influential ( )
   - (b) Slightly influential ( )
   - (c) Somewhat influential ( )
   - (d) Very influential ( )
   - (e) Extremely influential ( )

7. Is education affordable for all including indirect costs such as textbooks and uniforms?
   - (a) Never ( )
   - (b) Rarely ( )
   - (c) Sometimes ( )
   - (d) Often ( )
   - (e) Always ( )

8. Are you satisfied with the present method of recruitment of teachers?
   - (a) Not at all satisfied ( )
   - (b) Slightly satisfied ( )
   - (c) Moderately satisfied ( )
   - (d) Very satisfied ( )
   - (e) Extremely satisfied ( )

9. Are the teachers being deputed for in-service training?
   - (a) Never ( )
   - (b) Rarely ( )
   - (c) Sometimes ( )
   - (d) Often ( )
   - (e) Always ( )

Part – IV: To Identify the Possibilities of an Accountable Educational Administration

Accountability: *Accountability is a key to the successful school system, and therefore must be fair and transparent; teachers' accountability to their employers, to their students, or to parents - affects what they are willing to attempt, while their degree of autonomy impacts their ability to adapt content and methods to local needs.

1. What procedure do you follow for admission of students in your School?
   (a) Personal Interview ( )
   (b) Written Test ( )
   (c) Oral Test ( )
   (d) Both written and oral test ( )
   (e) Any other ( )
2. Is there any Managing Committee in your school?
   (a) Not at all influential ( )
   (b) Slightly influential ( )
   (c) Somewhat influential ( )
   (d) Very influential ( )
   (e) Extremely influential ( )
3. Does the Managing Committee hold the meetings regularly?
   (a) Never ( )
   (b) Rarely ( )
   (c) Sometimes ( )
   (d) Often ( )
   (e) Always ( )
4. Do you have a Parent - Teacher Association in your school?
   (a) Not at all influential ( )
   (b) Slightly influential ( )
   (c) Somewhat influential ( )
   (d) Very influential ( )
   (e) Extremely influential ( )
5. Does the Inspector of School come to visit your school?
   (a) Never ( )
   (b) Rarely ( )
   (c) Sometimes ( )
   (d) Often ( )
   (e) Always ( )

6. When was your school inspected last?
   - (a) 12-24 months ago ( )
   - (b) 9-12 months ago ( )
   - (c) 6-9 months ago ( )
   - (d) 3-6 months ago ( )
   - (e) 0-3 months ago ( )
7. In these options, which you do not keep in your school office?
   - (a) Admission register ( )
   - (b) Attendance register ( )
   - (c) Transfer and leaving certificate register ( )
   - (d) Guardians' meeting proceeding register ( )
   - (e) Any other ( )
8. How satisfied are you with your teaching job?
   - (a) Not at all satisfied ( )
   - (b) Slightly satisfied ( )
   - (c) Moderately satisfied ( )
   - (d) Very satisfied ( )
   - (e) Extremely satisfied ( )
9. Please tick any one of the following type of financial assistance that your school is receiving from the Government.
   - (a) Maintenance grants ( )
   - (b) Salary for the teachers ( )
   - (c) Scholarship for students ( )
   - (d) Any other ( )
   - (e) No grants ( )
10. Do you get financial assistance in time?
    - (a) Never ( )
    - (b) Rarely ( )
    - (c) Sometimes ( )
    - (d) Often ( )
    - (e) Always ( )
11. Does your school follow the maintenance of regularity and punctuality of teachers and administrators?
    - (a) Never ( )
    - (b) Rarely ( )

(c) Sometimes ( )

(d) Often ( )

(e) Always ( )

12. What do you think about the administrative problems of your child's school?
____
____

13. Academic problems ____________________
____

14. Financial problems ____________________
____

15. Any other (please specify) ____________________
____
____

16. What is your opinion about the standard of primary education? (Please state)
____
____
____
____

Index

H

I

J

K

L

M

N

O

P

Q

R

S

T